MW01193521

Selling
the
Stairway
to
Heaven

Critiquing the Claims of Heaven Tourists

Jim Osman

This book is self-published by James C. Osman II and
Kootenai Community Church Publishing.

ISBN: 978-0-692-53560-8

Cover artwork provided by Jason Duchow at
http://www.jasonduchowphotography.com

Website hosting provided by Thomas Leo at
http://www.TLCWebHosting.com

Visit the ministry of Kootenai Community Church at
http://www.KootenaiChurch.org
http://www.TruthOrTerritory.com

Selling the Stairway to Heaven

Dedication

This book is dedicated to the loving, joy-filled, faithful saints that gather as Kootenai Community Church who make it a joy to serve as an undershepherd of Jesus Christ.

Table of Contents

Acknowledgments

No list of acknowledgments for any book can ever be complete. There are so many people who have given me feedback, asked questions, and offered encouragement to me because of the chapters you find in this book. I feel obligated to list them all and thank them publicly, but that is impossible.

I am indebted to those who have had an editorial hand in this work: my secretary Marcia Whetsel and copy editor Jenny Leo. I am especially grateful and indebted to my wife, Diedre, who has pored over these pages with all the love any man could expect from his bride. Her attention to detail keeps me from looking like an idiot and she has spent more time proofing and editing these pages than I did writing them. Thank you, Sweety.

I am grateful to God for the congregation of Kootenai Community Church, composed of saints who love the truth and examine everything I say in its light. What a joy it has been to worship and serve the Lord with those believers for the last 20+ years. I praise God for the elders and deacons of this local body of Christ. The leadership of this congregation are godly men whom I consider it a joy to count among my closest friends. May God grant us many years of fruitful and faithful service together.

Thank you, Jason, Son of Duchow, Master of Graphics (jasonduchowphotography.com) for your work on the cover. You are a busy man and I am grateful you took the time to help me out.

Last, but certainly not least, thank you, dear reader, for buying this book and taking the time to read it. I pray that these chapters will serve to bless and challenge you and bring you closer to Christ our King.

Soli Deo Gloria!

Without Wax-
Jim Osman

Introduction

People are fascinated with the afterlife. Mankind seems hardwired with a longing for eternity (Ecclesiastes 3:11), a desire to live forever, and to know, with some degree of certainty, what awaits us after we pass through the veil at the end of life. It is no surprise that when books which purport to tell the story of a trip to Heaven[1] are published, they fly off the shelves of Christian bookstores and distributors almost as fast as they can be printed.

Heaven visitations are all the rage today. A retelling of the sights, sounds, and smells of a supposed trip to Heaven can land an author at the top of the bestseller list and produce enough speaking engagements, morning television appearances, news segments, and interviews on Christian TV and radio to keep him at the top of the bestseller list for quite some time. Churches are not the only fertile soil for marketing their wares. Fox News, CNN, ABC, and nearly every other major media outlet - including talk radio - have featured interviews and stories with those who claim to have visited Heaven. There is almost no surer way of inking a lucrative book deal than to offer even a moderately believable account of a visit to Heaven. Without even a modicum of discernment, Christian publishers gobble up such fare in hopes of making millions. Touring Heaven has proven to be big business.

Don Piper[2] got it started with his book *90 Minutes in Heaven* which has sold more than four million copies in over twenty-two languages.[3] Not to be outdone, Colton Burpo's account, *Heaven Is for Real,* has surpassed six million copies in sales. Apparently people are hungry for confirmation of the Bible's teaching concerning the afterlife. This desire for

1

experiences which confirm the Bible's message is one indicator of the insipid state of modern evangelicalism.

Todd Burpo's book, *Heaven Is for Real*, has been made into a major motion picture by Sony; and as I write this, Piper's book, *90 Minutes in Heaven*, is in production for the big screen.

Why This Review

For a long time I have ignored these authors and the books they wrote hoping that each title published would be the last. The increasing sales figures indicate that this is no passing fad. It appears that we can expect much more from this genre in the years to come.

Why would someone who loves the truth and desires to see the advance of the gospel write a book critiquing the claims of those who offer first-hand accounts of visits to Heaven? The answer is, because he loves the truth and desires to see the advance of the gospel. The modern-day reports of Heaven tourism advance neither of these ends.

Surely such publicity and name recognition should be good for the gospel, shouldn't it? Shouldn't we as Christians be excited to see people offering proof of Heaven, and proof of the Bible's truthfulness? Doesn't this serve as a great apologetic for the faith?

Actually, no. In this book I will show that modern reports of visits to Heaven actually do positive harm to the Body of Christ, and only serve to undermine the credibility of Scripture. I understand that that is quite a claim. I also understand that that is the opposite of what we are told by many Christian leaders, even very well-meaning ones. But it is a claim that I believe is backed up by the chapters you are about to read.

In conversations with various Christians who have read these books, I find people respond a number of different ways:

Unquestioning Confidence: Some find the source of hope that the author intends - an experience confirming the Bible's testimony. They delight to read a first-hand account which seems to increase their hunger for Heaven and their love for Jesus. They do not question the truthfulness of the account, fearing it would be on par with questioning the reality of God Himself or the reliability of His Word.

Why question something that confirms the Scriptures? Shouldn't we be delighted we have yet another confirmation the Bible is true and trustworthy? Why criticize evidence that supports my worldview and lends credibility to God's Word?

Undiscerning Curiosity: Some respond with, "I don't know if it happened or not, but wouldn't it be cool if it did?" Failing to see the danger with these books or spot theological problems, they are titillated by the accounts. They are excited to read of someone's experience, thinking they can glean some truth or find some confirmation of what they find in Scripture.

These folks are not necessarily convinced that what they are reading is completely true, but neither do they care. They are reading of an experience that confirms their deepest-held beliefs. Isn't that a good thing?

Unconvinced Criticism: Me. I am not at all convinced that Don Piper, Colton Burpo, or Eben Alexander have visited Heaven.

It is my hope that publishing critical theological reviews of three bestsellers will help demonstrate some of the serious flaws and theological problems with these books. I trust that by exposing error, the hearts of God's

3

people will be turned to the truth of Scripture, and they may be equipped to discern the dangers present with these supposed accounts.

The following chapters offer critiques of three popular bestsellers: *90 Minutes in Heaven*, *Heaven Is for Real*, and *Proof of Heaven*. The first two are written by professing Christians. My critiques of these two books contrast their claims with Scripture. The third book was written by a self-proclaimed pagan. I examined all three books for internal consistency. I have offered citations of their books, as well as media appearances. I have tried to be diligent to footnote every claim so the reader can examine my citations and draw their own conclusions.

The last two chapters offer a summary of the problems with all modern claims of visits to Heaven and a presentation of the true gospel.

It is my genuine desire that the Lord of the Church may use these reviews and critiques to establish His people in the faith once for all delivered to the saints (Jude 3). I pray that God may reform His church and call His people back to a firm conviction of and rest in the sufficiency of Scripture. I long for the day when no Christian will be deceived and tricked by the cleverly devised fables of modern charlatans. That day cannot come soon enough!

Note: Throughout the course of this critique, I have included page numbers of citations in brackets (pg) so the reader can easily double-check my citations with the original sources.

All the proceeds from the sale of this book will go to the building fund of Kootenai Community Church to help finish our new facility. Thank you for your support!

Endnotes

1. The reader may notice throughout this review that sometimes the word "Heaven" is capitalized and sometimes it is not. I prefer to capitalize the word since "Heaven" is a proper noun describing an actual place like Cleveland or Miami. However, Piper does not capitalize it (according to conventional standards) so when quoting him, it will remain uncapitalized.

2. Don Piper should not be confused with John Piper of Desiring God Ministries. As far as I know, there is no relation.

3. http://www.donpiperministries.com/intl_publishers.asp lists twenty-two foreign languages in which the book can be purchased. Sales figure taken from http://www.challies.com/articles/heaven-tourism.

A Critical Theological Review of *90 Minutes in Heaven* by Don Piper

On January 18, 1989, Pastor Don Piper claims that he died in an auto accident on a narrow bridge in Texas. While traveling home to Alvin, Texas from a BGCT[1] conference held on the north shore of Lake Livingston via I-45 in a rainstorm, Piper was struck head-on by an eighteen-wheeler. The truck, driven by an inmate, a trustee at the Texas Department of Corrections, weaved across the center line, colliding with Don Piper's Ford Escort. According to the accident report, the impact was about 110 miles per hour. Piper's car was crushed under the wheels of the heavy truck.

Piper reports:

According to those who were at the scene, the guards called for medical backup from the prison, and they arrived a few minutes later. Someone examined me, found no pulse, and declared that I had been killed instantly.

I have no recollection of the impact or anything that happened afterward.

In one powerful, overwhelming second, I died (20).[2]

Further, Piper claims that EMTs at the scene of the collision checked his pulse twice - once at 11:45 a.m. and then again at 1:15 p.m. Both times, EMTs confirmed that he was dead.

Almost ninety minutes after the collision, another conference attendee, Dick Onerecker, arrived at the scene and took his place in the long line of backed-up traffic. After some time he approached the scene of the accident and said to a police officer, "I'm a minister. Is there anyone here I can help? Is there anyone I can pray for?" (41).

Though he had already been informed that Piper was dead, Dick felt led to pray over his dead body (42). As Dick began to sing "What a Friend We Have In Jesus," Piper returned to life and consciousness and began to sing along.

Dick quickly summoned an EMT who refused to believe that the "dead man" was now alive. The EMT went and checked on Piper, and this time he found a pulse. Medical personnel rushed into action to extract Piper's mangled body from the wreckage and rush him to the nearest hospital. Then began the long and painful healing and recovery.

During the ninety minutes that elapsed between the impact of the accident and Piper returning to life, he claims that he visited Heaven. The book purports to tell that story.

A Needed Clarification

Fifty years ago, I would not have needed to say what immediately follows. However, in today's world, any criticism of someone's writing, story, or beliefs is automatically assumed to be an ad hominem[3] attack. Examining someone's theology or experience in the light of Scripture is no longer deemed a noble enterprise (Acts 17:11). People assume that any criticism of somebody else, particularly if they have endured a tragedy, can only be motivated by lack of compassion, personal hatred, or some form of bigotry.

I assure you that is not the case. I have never met Mr. Piper. I have never gone to any of his speaking engagements, nor have I read any of his books or writings except *90 Minutes in Heaven*.

The concerns that I must raise have to do with the theology, the contents, and the underlying assumptions contained in his book.

As I read the book, my heart was truly wrenched by the amount of pain and suffering that Mr. Piper endured. Today he lives with pain and disability which still linger from the accident. He has not regained full use of his limbs, and the limitations are real and substantial. I do not doubt any of that, nor do I wish anything of what he has endured on any person, living or dead.

I believe Mr. Piper is probably a very gracious man, kind, a great husband, and a good father. However, I also believe that the statements and assumptions of *90 Minutes in Heaven* deserve a thorough theological response. Despite his intentions, I believe that his story and others like it are detrimental to the faith and ministry of the Church.

Some readers will assume that I'm cold-hearted and lacking basic compassion to publish a criticism of a man who has suffered so much already. However, no amount of suffering makes someone immune to criticism. I can and do sympathize with Mr. Piper's physical disabilities while at the same time express grave concern over his "story."

Mr. Piper has gone on the record and published the details of something that he believes was personally revealed to him by God. He promotes his books and tapes through various speaking engagements, his website, as well as other venues. He encourages Christians to not only read

9

his book, but accept it as truth - gospel truth - and an authentication of the Bible's teachings. He advises us to take him at his word and to derive hope and encouragement from it. In fact, he claims that because of his firsthand knowledge of Heaven, he is able to prepare you and me for it (190).

Piper has made theological statements and claims. The book itself claims to be an account of a first-hand revelation of the realities of Heaven. Having sold four million copies, his book has had an immeasurable impact in the Church; therefore, his teachings, his claims, and his assumptions deserve to be examined closely.

A Healthy Skepticism

Piper admits to skepticism regarding other people's claims of visiting Heaven. Having watched others on TV relate their near-death experiences, he admits:

I confess to being fascinated, but I also admit to being skeptical. In fact, I'm highly skeptical. Before and after those people spoke, I thought, "They've probably had some kind of brain lapse. Or maybe there was already something in their memory bank and they just re-experienced it." I didn't doubt their sincerity; they wanted to believe what they talked about.

I've watched many talk shows and read about victims who had died and been heroically resuscitated. Descriptions of their ordeals often seem too rehearsed and disturbingly similar, as if one person copied the story of the last. One person who claimed to have been dead for more than twenty-four hours wrote a book and said he had talked to Adam and Eve. Some of the things the

10

first earthly couple purportedly told him don't measure up with the Bible (199-200).

I would suggest the same standard Mr. Piper applies to judge other claims of heavenly visitations should be applied to his own. Measuring Piper's claims concerning Heaven against the Bible's teaching will show that his claims are equally spurious.

Piper tries to place his experience above any skepticism or criticism when he says, "I have never questioned my own death" (200). Further he asserts:

> In the same way, some may not believe my account; they may think it was some kind of wish fulfillment during a point of severe trauma. **I don't have to defend my experience.**[4] I know what happened to me. For those of us whose faith is in the reality of heaven, no amount of evidence is necessary. I know what I experienced (205).

Those words, whether intentional or not, place Piper's claims above criticism. What does it say of you if you are skeptical and doubt the validity of his story? Does that mean that your faith is not in the reality of Heaven?

I would respectfully disagree with Piper's assertion. He cannot claim that his experience is proof of the Bible's teaching, gives him credibility, should be a source of hope and encouragement to others, is a private, modern-day revelation, and at the same time claim that he does not need to defend his experience. No experience is above defending. I assume that Mr. Piper would not say that his faith in Christ, the doctrine of the bodily resurrection, the Scripture, or the truth should not be defended. Why does he think that his story does not need to be defended? He is called to defend the faith once for all delivered to the saints (Jude 3), but his experience is above that? Why are we to believe his experience is somehow immune to criticism and above skepticism? Piper expects you to take him at his word and believe him uncritically.

A Paucity of Information

Given the title, *90 Minutes in Heaven*, we might expect the bulk of the book to be a recounting of his time spent there. If you purchased the book hoping to get 205 pages of firsthand knowledge concerning Heaven, you will be sorely disappointed. Of course, by the time you realize that, you will have already purchased the book!

The most striking feature of the book is the total paucity of information on the subject which is in the title of the book, namely, Heaven. Of the 205 pages, only fifteen are spent describing his ninety minutes there. The rest is a detailed and painstaking account of his accident, trip to the hospital, time in the hospital, release from the hospital, recovery, pain, suffering, medications, treatments, visitors, continuing physical disabilities, struggle with whether or not to go public with his experience, and accounts of all the people who have benefited from his descriptions of Heaven. After reading the entire book, I can say that I learned more about the Ilizarov device[5] which was attached to his left leg than I did about Heaven!

Ninety percent of the book is not even about Heaven. Apart from the occasional reminder of his time there (78, 79, 102, 123), there are only fifteen pages of the book dedicated to describing this place which Piper claims was "the most real thing that has ever happened to me."[6] He says, "Everything I experienced was like a first-class buffet for the senses" (25), and, "In heaven, each of our senses is immeasurably heightened to take it all in. And what a

12

sensory celebration!" (28). Yet, the amount of detail provided in the book about Heaven would not suggest that this was "the most real thing that has ever happened" to him. He is not short on detail about those who prayed for his recovery, the Ilizarov device, the pain he experienced, medications he took, or the lessons he learned. But when it comes to "the most real thing that has ever happened" to him, strikingly little is said.

Piper could have easily written a book detailing God's answer to the prayers of His people. That would've made a great testimony, and one of tremendous encouragement to believers. The book could have been an account of one man's struggle to survive and find purpose in suffering. That would have been a helpful book. It could have been the story of one man's triumph over adversity, depression, and pain. That would have been an encouragement to many Christians. Absent the fifteen pages describing Piper's experience of Heaven, the book could have proven to be useful.

However, I am certain it would not have sold four million copies. Neither would Piper have been featured on TBN, ABC, and offered numerous speaking engagements. Without the claim to offer first-hand knowledge of Heaven, the book would not sell and this review would not have been written.

So why is Piper's account of Heaven not more robust? Why is the bulk of the book not about the very subject that its title suggests?

The skeptic in me wonders if Piper knows that the only thing that makes his story remarkable, and thus marketable, is his purported experience of Heaven. Is Piper afraid that offering too much detail might put him in a position of contradicting either himself or Scripture? After all, when you are making up a story, it is easier to keep it straight if you keep it simple.

Remember, his skepticism regarding other near-death experiences is based upon the fact that "descriptions of their ordeals often seem too rehearsed and disturbingly similar, as if one person copied the story of the last" (199-200). Ironically, that is exactly how Piper's account strikes me. His description is banal, generic, superficial, and lacking in details. It is exactly the kind of description you might expect from anyone who tries to imagine what Heaven would be like and is disturbingly similar to other accounts. As Tim Challies writes, "If you were to ask your unbelieving friends and neighbors to describe heaven, they would probably create a place very much like this."[7]

On With the Critique!

For the sake of organization, I'll address the dangers of this book under four headings: Piper's Claims about Heaven, Miscellaneous Theological Concerns, Gospel Presentation, and Piper's View of Scripture.

Criticism #1:
Piper's Claims about Heaven

No Jesus

Only two short chapters of the book are given to describing Piper's time in Heaven, and much of that is spent recalling details from his childhood and telling the stories of the people he met when he arrived in Heaven.

Chapter 2, titled *My Time in Heaven*, describes the sights, the people, and the feelings of being in Heaven. Chapter 3, titled *Heavenly Music*, is given to describe the worship music of Heaven and the reason that **Piper did not see God** (33) during his ninety minutes there.

14

Numerous times in these two chapters Piper tells us that he did not actually get to pass through the gates of Heaven into Heaven itself. Everything that he experienced was outside Heaven's gates.[8] Before he ever stepped inside, he was sent back to the wreckage of his body and his Ford Escort (36).

His first memory of Heaven is seeing a large crowd of people "in front of a brilliant, ornate gate." They had gathered "just outside heaven's gate, waiting for me" (22). Piper never actually went inside Heaven. All he saw, heard and felt was outside Heaven's gate. The book should be titled *90 Minutes Outside of Heaven's Gate*. It is not unfair to say that Piper has no idea what it is like to spend ninety minutes in Heaven, since by his own account, he never set foot inside.

The fact that Piper never actually went into Heaven explains why he can affirm that he never actually saw Jesus or God the Father. He writes, "As the crowd rushed toward me, I didn't see Jesus, but I did see people I had known" (22). Elsewhere, Piper says again, "I did not see God. Although I knew God was there, I never saw any kind of image or luminous glow to indicate his divine presence" (33).

Piper explains why he believes that he didn't actually get to see God:

> The only way I've made sense out of that part of the experience is to think that if I had actually seen God, I would never have wanted to return. My feeling has been that once we're actually in God's presence, we will never return to earth again, because it will be empty and meaningless by comparison (33).

One wonders how the sights and sounds, the deep joy, the knowledge, the reunion with loved ones, the music, the food, the freedom from pain, anxiety, and sin is not enough to make this earth feel empty and meaningless by comparison!

This absence of the presence of God is one of the most glaring problems with Piper's account. How is it possible that one can spend ninety minutes waiting outside of Heaven without ever seeing Jesus? What is the source of Heaven's joy and contentment if not the very presence of the risen Christ? Piper describes a glory and joy, a "buffet for the senses," a "sensory celebration" (28), and feeling "perfect love" (27). He says, "All worries, anxieties, and concerns vanished. I had no needs, and I felt perfect" (33) - all without ever seeing Jesus or being in the presence of God. The "Heaven" that Piper describes is fulfilling, peaceful, joyful, loving, and alluring, **even without seeing Jesus**.

John Piper (no relation) in his book, *God is the Gospel*, asks this searching question:

> If you could have heaven, with no sickness, and with all the friends you ever had on earth, and all the food you ever liked, and all the leisure activities you ever enjoyed, and all the natural beauties you ever saw, all the physical pleasures you ever tasted, and no human conflict or any natural disasters, could you be satisfied with heaven, if Christ were not there?[9]

According to *90 Minutes in Heaven* the answer is a resounding YES!

Ironically, even while claiming that he spent ninety minutes in Heaven without seeing Jesus, Piper says:

> As a pastor, I've stood at the foot of many caskets

and done many funerals and said, "To be absent from the body is to be present with the Lord to those who love him and know him." I believed those words before. I believe them even more now (34).

How can he believe those words even more now since, by his own account, he was absent from the body for ninety minutes and yet never entered into the presence of the Lord?

The contradictions on this central point do not stop there. Justin Peters (justinpeters.org) recounts the following in his online review of Piper's book:

On March 29 of this year, my wife and I went to see Don Piper speak at First Baptist Church of Bristow, OK. Having read his book, I was quite surprised to hear him say that, in fact, he did see God "way down the golden road up on a hill on His throne."[10] This is a huge discrepancy. Wanting to make sure I did not misunderstand, I talked to him after the service and asked him why he said in his book that he did not see God when he now says that he did.

Piper: Really in the distance, yes, in the distance I saw Him.

Peters: But in *90 Minutes in Heaven* you said, "I did not see God."

Piper: I'm telling you now that I did.

Peters: OK, so why did you say in the book you didn't?

Piper: I didn't say I didn't see Him. I, I, I, I was

looking from a distance through the gate. You could see the golden street, you could see the buildings, there are mansions, and you could see a hill with a river flowing down the side of it. . . . It was just so personal to me and so incredibly difficult to describe [that] I just didn't include that. And that's one of the things I did not include. Let me tell you something, I didn't write the book by myself. I had a co-writer who writes. His name is Cec Murphy. So, there are probably some things in there that he interpreted differently than I did and that may be one of them.[11]

It is truly difficult to imagine anything more real and memorable than seeing God, yet Piper leaves this out of his account and is directly contradicted by his own book. This is not just a mere oversight.

Sights, Sounds, and Feelings

Piper claims:

Everything I experienced was like a first-class buffet for the senses. I had never felt such powerful embraces or feasted my eyes on such beauty. Heaven's light and texture defied earthly eyes or explanation. Warm, radiant light engulfed me. As I looked around, I could hardly grasp the vivid, dazzling colors. Every hue and tone surpassed anything I had ever seen (25).

He describes being enveloped "with a brilliance beyond earthly comprehension or description" (21). Things were "brilliantly intense," "utterly luminous," a "brilliance that was brighter than the light that surrounded us" (27), and a "bright iridescence" (33).

18

Piper describes the joy of Heaven (26) and a love that "emanated from every person who surrounded [him]" (27). He laments the limits of "earthly terms to refer to unimaginable joy, excitement, warmth, and total happiness" (24). The music that he heard filled his heart with "the deepest joy I've ever experienced" and he felt the "joy and exuberance" of the heavenly worship (31). "Hymns of praise, modern-sounding choruses, and ancient chants filled my ears and brought not only a deep peace but the greatest feeling of joy I've ever experienced" (31). Remember, all of this without ever seeing Jesus!

Contradictory Statements - Memory

Piper repeatedly claims his experience in Heaven was lived out in a heightened state of awareness and knowledge. Consider the following:

"Everything I experienced was like a first-class buffet for the senses. . . . With all the heightened awareness of my senses, I felt as if I had never seen, heard, or felt anything so real before" (25).

"In heaven, each of our senses is immeasurably heightened to take it all in. And what a sensory celebration!" (28).

"Maybe it was because my senses were so engaged that I feasted on everything at the same time" (30).

In an interview on ABC, Piper said going to Heaven was "the most real thing that has ever happened to me."[12]

Yet despite the fact that his senses were "immeasurably heightened to take it all in," there is so much that he doesn't seem to recall. It seems that the only thing imperfect about him during his ninety minutes in Heaven is his memory.

For instance, the first person Piper supposedly saw was his grandfather. Upon seeing him, Piper confesses, "I may have called his name, but *I'm not sure.* After being hugged by my grandfather, *I don't remember* who was second or third" (23). He says that people were excited and overjoyed to see him, but "*I'm not sure* if they actually said the words or not, but I knew they had been waiting and expecting me" (25).

When feeling love from those who welcomed him, he writes, "They didn't say they loved me. *I don't remember* what words they spoke" (27). But he felt it emanate from them.

One glaring contradiction occurs in two sentences right next to each other:

> With all the heightened awareness of my senses, I felt as if I had never seen, heard, or felt anything so real before. *I don't recall* that I tasted anything, yet I knew that if I had, that too would have been more glorious than anything I had eaten or drunk on earth.

He has never experienced anything so real before, but he can't recall if he ate anything. That is a lot of uncertainty and lack of memory for someone whose senses were "immeasurably heightened" so he could "take it all in" during the "most real thing that has ever happened" to him.

Contradictory Statements - Knowledge

Piper claims that while in Heaven, "I asked no questions and never wondered about anything. Everything was perfect. I sensed that I knew everything and had no questions to ask" (30).

There are a few things Piper seems to have intuitively known. For instance, ". . . I also knew that in heaven there is

20

no sense of time passing" (25). He knew that those selected to welcome him to Heaven had been selected because of the spiritual impact they had on him in this life. "I knew - again one of those things I knew without being aware of how I had absorbed that information - that because of their influence I was able to be present with them in heaven" (26). "No one said it, but I simply knew God had sent all those people to escort me inside the portals of heaven" (34). Though he never saw angels, he did hear the "swishing" of their wings. "As I listened I simply knew what it was" (30).

Yet for someone who sensed that he knew everything and had no questions, he sure confesses to have not known a lot! He wasn't sure of the nature of the music he heard, whether it was a voice or something instrumental (30-31). He did not even know who was singing the glorious music - angels or humans (31). He didn't know why his grandfather was the first person he saw (23). He had no idea how old some people were in Heaven (26). He did not know how many songs were being sung simultaneously in Heaven (32). When asked, "How did you move? Did you walk? Did you float?" Piper responds, "I don't know" (35).

That is a whole lot of **not knowing** for someone who sensed he knew everything. It is a lot of unanswered questions for someone who "had no questions to ask" (30).

Contradictory Statements - Pain

Piper highlights one person in his "greeting committee" who was a childhood friend. This particular friend was killed in a car wreck after high school. He writes:

> When I attended his funeral, I wondered if I would ever stop crying. . . .Through the years since then, I had never been able to forget the pain and sense of loss. Not that I thought of him all the time, but when I did, sadness came over me. . . .

21

Now I saw Mike in heaven. As he slipped his arm around my shoulder, my pain and grief vanished (23).

Piper seems to be saying that even while in Heaven he was aware of the pain and grief that accompanied that memory until Mike put his arm around him. Only then did that grief vanish.

In spite of the fact that he recounts feeling this pain and grief while in Heaven, Piper later records:

I wasn't conscious of anything I'd left behind and felt no regrets about leaving family or possessions. It was as if God had removed anything negative or worrisome from my consciousness, and I could only rejoice at being together with these wonderful people (26).

Oh yeah, except there was that pain and grief over Mike that didn't vanish until some time into the ninety minutes.

Misplaced Hope - A Big Family Reunion

Piper tries to paint a picture of Heaven intended to thrill us with anticipation. Yet, as already noted, he leaves out the most thrilling part of Heaven - Jesus. The appeal of Piper's Heaven seems to come from the hope of being with people we knew in this life.

A great deal of time is spent recounting how thrilled people were to see him and how joyful he was to see people like his grandfather, his friend Mike, and his great-grandmother, Hattie Mann. The predominant highlight of his ninety minutes centers around these people. Piper writes, "He and everyone that followed praised God and told me how excited they were to see me and to welcome me to heaven and to the fellowship they enjoyed" (24).

All the Piper family reunions at the park in Monticello, Arkansas paled in comparison to this reunion.

None of those earthly family reunions, however, prepared me for the sublime gathering of saints I experienced at the gates of heaven. Those who had gathered at Monticello were some of the same people waiting for me at the gates of heaven. Heaven was many things, but without a doubt, it was the greatest family reunion of all (25).

What did they talk about? "Our conversations centered on the joy of my being there and how happy they were to see me" (26). He describes being with the people as "the most human warmth and friendliness I've ever witnessed. Just being with them was a holy moment and remains a treasured hope" (27).

What is Piper's "treasured hope?" Being with his departed loved ones. What about Jesus? What about God?

That is the joy of Piper's Heaven - a family reunion where the conversation centers on the joy of being there and being so happy to see each other again. I guess that is all you have when Jesus is conspicuously absent. The real joy of Heaven will be the glory and presence of Christ - even without our loved ones! (2 Corinthians 5:1-9; Philippians 1:21).

Yet, even the family reunion is not what Piper looks forward to most. In Chapter 3, which describes the music of Heaven, Piper confesses:

As I've pondered the meaning of the memory of the music, it seems curious. I would have expected the most memorable experience to be something I had seen or the physical embrace of a loved one. Yet **above everything else, I cherish** those sounds, and at times I think, **I can't wait to hear them**

23

again - in person. It's what I look forward to. I want to see everybody, but I know I'll be with them forever. I want to experience everything heaven offers, **but most of all**, I want to hear those never ending songs again.[13]

This is Piper's Heaven. The deepest sense of joy comes not from being in God's presence and coming to know Him, but from being welcomed by family and friends who have already gone to Heaven. According to Piper, that which we have to anticipate above all else is not seeing Jesus and bowing before Him, but hearing the music of Heaven. This is a pathetically low, sad, man-centered, Christ-less view of Heaven and its joys. It offers thrills and excitements which are superficial, shallow, banal, and childish - excitements which would appeal to only the most immature of Christians. Then again, that certainly appears to be his intended audience.

Age in Heaven

Piper makes some claims about the ravages of age upon those in Heaven.

The first person he recognized in Heaven was his grandfather, Joe Kulbeth. Piper claims, "He looked exactly as I remembered him, with his shock of white hair and what I called a big banana nose" (22). The "white hair" appears to be an indicator of age.

Piper later claims, "I became aware of the wide variety of ages - old and young and every age in-between" (24).

Then, when Piper saw his great-grandmother, Hattie Mann, he noticed that "she stood strong and upright, and the wrinkles had been erased from her face. I have no idea what age she was, and I didn't even think about that. As I

24

stared at her beaming face, I sensed that age has no meaning in heaven" (26).

In an equally confusing explanation, Piper says:

Age expresses time passing, and there is no time there. All of the people I encountered were the same age they had been the last time I had seen them - except that all the ravages of living on earth had vanished (27).

So which is it? Does everyone have varying ages that we recognize and are aware of, or does age have no meaning in Heaven? How is it that he was aware of different ages and yet didn't even think about age since it had no meaning? If age has no meaning, how did he know they were the same age as when they departed earth?

Isn't age a ravage of living on earth? He wants to say that age has no meaning, but then he comments on the varying ages of the people he met and how their age appeared in Heaven. This is such convoluted, contradictory nonsense as to make one wonder why anyone would take it seriously.

No Time in Heaven

Repeatedly, Piper makes the claim that there is no time in Heaven. For instance:

"Time had no meaning" (24).

". . . yet I also knew that in heaven there is no sense of time passing" (25).

"Age expresses time passing, and there is no time there" (27).

"In those minutes - and they held no sense of time for me - others touched me" (33).

"For them, time is not passing. Everything is in the eternal now - even if I can't put that into words. Even if ten more years pass, or thirty, in heaven it will be only an instant before I'm back there again" (196).

If Piper had read Revelation before fabricating his story, he might not have made this elementary mistake. The present Heaven does experience time. In John's inspired record of his actual revelation of the real Heaven, he writes:

> When the Lamb broke the fifth seal, I saw underneath the altar the souls of those who had been slain because of the word of God, and because of the testimony which they had maintained; and they cried out with a loud voice, saying, "How long, O Lord, holy and true, will You refrain from judging and avenging our blood on those who dwell on the earth?" And there was given to each of them a white robe; and they were told that they should rest for a little while longer, until the number of their fellow servants and their brethren who were to be killed even as they had been, would be completed also (Revelation 6:9–11).[14]

The martyred saints in Heaven are clearly aware that time is passing on earth and in Heaven. In fact, the question that they ask only makes sense if they are well aware of time passing between their martyrdom and the execution of the just judgment of God. That is why they ask the question, "How long?" That is a time question.

The answer that the saints got is also a time-related answer. They were told that they should "rest for a little while longer." So much for time having no meaning in Heaven. Piper claims that in Heaven there is no sense of time passing. John, the inspired apostle, disagrees.

This is sufficient to show that either Piper has been deceived in his "vision" or he is intentionally deceiving others, having fabricated the entire story out of whole cloth.

The Songs

Another glaring contradiction to Scripture is contained in Piper's claim concerning the type of music that is used in Heaven for worship. He writes:

> Many of the old hymns and choruses I had sung at various times in my life were part of the music - along with hundreds of songs I had never heard before. Hymns of praise, modern-sounding choruses, and ancient chants filled my ears and brought not only a deep peace but the greatest feeling of joy I've ever experienced.
>
> As I stood before the gate, I didn't think of it, but later I realized that I didn't hear such songs as "The Old Rugged Cross" or "The Nail-Scarred Hand." **None of the hymns that filled the air were about Jesus' sacrifice or death. I heard no sad songs and instinctively knew that there are no sad songs in heaven. Why would there be?** All were praises about Christ's reign as King of Kings and our joyful worship for all that he has done for us and how wonderful he is (31).[15]

There are a number of obvious problems with Piper's claim. First, is not the death and sacrifice of Jesus part of "all that he has done for us and how wonderful he is"? Does not His death demonstrate just how wonderful He is? And is not His death the theological center of what He has done on behalf of His people? He came to give His life as a ransom for many and to die on behalf of us - to bear the wrath of God in the place of sinners (Mark 10:45; 1 Peter 2:24-25).

27

How can the worship of Heaven not center around that redemptive purchase?

It seems that the Heaven Piper describes is not just absent Jesus, but a place utterly unconcerned with the crowning jewel of God's glory - the cross.

Second, Piper asserts there are no sad songs in Heaven and so they don't sing about the sacrificial death of Christ. Piper's thinking on this issue is more than a bit juvenile. Since when does singing about the sacrifice of Christ bring sadness? Why should it? Singing about the atoning work of the Divine Son on behalf of His people should fill our hearts with joy, thankfulness, and hope. Why would Heaven's view of that act bring feelings of sadness? Why would those in Heaven who have been brought there by the death of Christ feel sadness instead of joy and happiness when reflecting on that reality? They have a sinless, perfect perspective on that event. They see the glory of God, and know joy and rejoicing. They are experiencing the goodness of God, the vindication of His justice, and the fullness of His grace.

With obvious cognitive disconnect, Piper claims during one of his speaking engagements that Jesus is the only person in Heaven with scars. He then explains, "This is to remind the rest of us how we got there."[16]

But wouldn't that make us sad? If singing of His sacrifice would make me sad, how much more, seeing the very visible evidence of the cross and His death on it? Why are there no sad songs, but there are sad scars? If songs about the sacrifice of Christ would make me sad and keep me from appropriately rejoicing, what will the scars do if I am constantly reminded of what He did? If Piper were giving us an account of a true revelation of Heaven, we would not find these types of inconsistencies and contradictions.

28

Remembering and rejoicing in the sacrificial death of Christ will be part of our worship, which Piper would know if he had consulted an actual revelation of Heaven before writing his book.

Third, this assertion directly contradicts the inspired revelation of Heaven given through the Apostle John in the book of Revelation. Unlike Piper, John actually went to Heaven, saw the throne of God, and witnessed the worship in Heaven. Revelation 4-5 is the record of that worship.

John records that when the Lamb took the scroll, the four living creatures and the twenty-four elders fell down before the Lamb and sang a new song saying:

Worthy are You to take the book and to break its seals; for **You were slain, and purchased for God with Your blood men** from every tribe and tongue and people and nation. You have made them to be a kingdom of priests to our God; and they will reign upon the earth.[17]

Then John looked and he

heard the voice of many angels around the throne and the living creatures and the elders; and the number of them was myriads of myriads, and thousands of thousands, saying with a loud voice, "Worthy is the **Lamb that was slain** to receive power and riches and wisdom and might and honor and glory and blessing."[18]

According to Piper, they don't sing about the death or sacrifice of Jesus. According to Scripture, Heaven does sing praise to the Lamb who was slain, and the songs do mention the death and sacrifice of Jesus. In fact, according to Scripture, even the angels join in singing about the slaying of the Lamb. Who will you believe, Piper or Scripture?

This blatant contradiction of Scripture is enough to show that either Piper has knowingly fabricated his entire story, or he was deceived by what he saw. Whatever it was, it was not Heaven.

Fourth, not only does Scripture record worship in Heaven which celebrates the death of Christ, but the book of Revelation speaks consistently and constantly of Jesus in such a way as to commemorate and celebrate His sacrificial death.

One of the major themes of Revelation is the references to Jesus as "the Lamb." John uses that title thirty-two times in thirty verses in Revelation.[19] The very portrayal of Jesus as a Lamb in Revelation calls to mind His sacrifice. The central imagery of Heaven is the imagery of sacrifice!The first time that John mentions the Lamb in his vision of Heaven, he sees Him as "**a Lamb standing, as if slain.**"[20]

In Heaven, praises are sung to the Lamb and His death is celebrated in song without sadness (Revelation 5:8-12). Not only is the sacrifice of Christ mentioned in song, but it is also discussed among those in Heaven. One of the elders says to John concerning the martyred tribulation saints, "These are the ones who come out of the great tribulation, and they have washed their robes and made them white in the blood of the Lamb" (Revelation 7:14).

Later in John's vision, he heard a loud voice saying:

Now the salvation, and the power, and the kingdom of our God and the authority of His Christ have come, for the accuser of our brethren has been thrown down, he who accuses them before our God day and night. And they overcame him because of the blood of the Lamb (Revelation 12:11).

If every mention of the sacrifice of Christ can only bring sadness, then why will we celebrate the marriage supper of the Lamb? Why will we be referred to as "the bride, the wife of the Lamb"? (Revelation 19:7, 9, 21:9). If Piper is right, it should be called "the marriage supper of the reigning King."

According to Scripture, in Heaven, the imagery and celebration of the Lamb slain is ever present. According to Piper, it is entirely absent.

Apparently, he was made aware of this contradiction because recently his story has changed. During one of his talks at the First Chinese Baptist Church sometime in 2008,[21] Piper said:

You see, there are songs in Heaven about the old rugged cross and the blood of the lamb, but the songs I heard at the gates of Heaven were all glorifying God. All authentic worship is to glorify God, it is not for us. It's for Him.[22]

Criticism #2:
Miscellaneous Theological Concerns

Extra-Biblical Revelations

Piper's account of ninety minutes in Heaven amounts to an extra-biblical revelation. He believes that God has revealed the realities of Heaven to him just as authoritatively and reliably as He did to the Apostle John. Piper might eschew the label of "extra-biblical revelation" to describe his experience, but that is precisely what he is claiming. He is asserting that he knows truth about Heaven because he received a revelation of Heaven. Piper's account is a revelation from outside Scripture - that is extra-biblical revelation.

Given the fact that Piper believes Heaven was personally revealed to him, it should not surprise us to discover that he also teaches that God speaks outside of

Scripture through personal, private, discernible revelations to His people.

This is most clearly seen in Piper's account of how Dick Onerecker came upon the accident scene and was prompted to pray for Piper, allegedly a dead man for ninety minutes at the time.

According to Piper:

Dick would later tell it this way: "**God spoke to me** and said, 'You need to pray for the man in the red car.'" Dick was an outstanding Baptist preacher. Praying for a dead man certainly ran counter to his theology. [*Apparently, receiving direct revelations from God did not run counter to his theology.*] "I can't do that," he thought. "How can I go over there and pray? The man is dead."

Dick stared at the officer, knowing that what he would say wouldn't make sense. **Yet God spoke to him** so clearly that he had no doubt about what he was to do. **God had told him** to pray for a dead man. As bizarre as that seemed to him, Dick also had no doubt that **the Holy Spirit was prompting him** to act.

He began praying for me. As he said later, "I felt compelled to pray. I didn't know who the man was or whether he was a believer. **I knew only that God told me** I had to pray for him."

This sounds strange, because Dick knew I was dead. . . . He had no idea why he prayed as he did, except **God told him to** (42-43).[23]

Piper also claims to have heard the voice of God inside his head upon returning to church for the first time after the

32

A Critical Theological Review of 90 Minutes in Heaven by Don Piper

accident. When people applauded, Piper felt guilty about their applause and excitement. "**Then God spoke to me.** This was one of the few times in my life when I heard a **very clear voice inside my head.**" The voice informed him, "They're not applauding for you" (121).

Not only is a voice inside the head equated with divine revelation, but Piper speaks of following signs to discern God's desires. When debating whether or not to go public with his experience,[24] a friend challenged him to share parts of his experience with two trusted friends. If those friends thought he was crazy or had hallucinated, then Piper should never speak of it again.

"But if they rejoice with you," he said, "and if they urge you to tell them more, I want you to **take this as a sign - a sign** that God wants you to talk about those ninety minutes you spent in heaven" (127).[25]

I understand this is part of modern evangelical vernacular and the practice of a multitude of Christians. However, the practice of discerning the will and desires of God by signs is fraught with danger and deception. If Piper had compared his experience with Scripture, he would have been able to discern that God did not want him to share it since it contradicts Scripture. Piper should know that experiences are unreliable and no certain test of truth.

This belief in, and reliance upon, private, personal revelations is unbiblical and incompatible with a belief in the sufficiency of Scripture. It is just another of the problems with the theology that Piper presents in his book.

Miracles Confused

Piper continually uses imprecise theological language using the word "miracle" to speak of things which are not miracles at all. Piper justifies this imprecision by saying:

> I refer to them as miracles - although some may call them fortunate circumstances - because I believe there are no accidents or surprises with God (55).

Just because we believe that God is sovereign and omniscient does not mean that we are free to refer to any or every detail of our lives as "miracles," even if we can see the hand of God in them. As a minister, Piper should know better. If you call everything a miracle, then nothing is truly miraculous. Though he did experience displays of God's power, providence, grace, kindness, and reminders of God's goodness, these are not miracles.

For example, things that we might refer to as providence or explain by the natural healing processes of the human body, Piper calls "miracles." Recovering from pneumonia, the medical staff discovering a problem with a breathing tube (61), being able to make even the smallest improvements during the healing process (71), the lifting of depression (107), and his wife and children making it through a semester of school in spite of his tragedy (143), are all referred to as "miracles." The caring providence of God evident in the grace that He provided to make these realities happen might be noteworthy and certainly worthy of praise, but none of these fit the biblical definition of "miracle."

On page 73, Piper writes, "That's perhaps the biggest miracle: **People prayed and God honored their prayers**."[26] At best this is a gaffe! I believe it is truly a blessing and amazing that God answers prayer, but is it a miracle? No. The fact that God answers the prayers of His people is not a miracle. It is the *normal* way that God works on behalf of His people.

Don Piper, an ordained minister since 1985,[27] should know what constitutes a "miracle." Yet this type of

34

theological imprecision and inaccuracy plagues Piper's descriptions of God's workings in the midst of his suffering and only serves to confuse the reader.

Criticism #3:
Gospel Presentation

It is tremendously disappointing to read a book that purports to be about Heaven which fails to give any clear presentation of how to get there. In fact, there is no discernible gospel presentation in the pages of this book. **None.**

I would imagine that if I had been to Heaven and seen the glories of the life to come, I would become exponentially more passionate about the gospel, presenting the gospel, and telling everyone I could about the gospel than I am today. In fact, I would imagine that the only thing I would be able to talk about would be the gospel of God's glorious grace. Yet, somehow Piper could not find a means of working the gospel into the pages of this book - a sad fact given that four million copies have been sold.

One might have expected the gospel to take center stage given what Piper says about wanting people to go there.

> Third, I want as many people as possible to go to heaven. I've always believed Christian theology that declares heaven is real and a place for God's people. Since my own experience of having been there, **I've felt a stronger sense of responsibility to <u>make the way absolutely clear</u>**. Not only do I want people to go to heaven, I now feel an urgency about helping them open their lives so they can be assured that's where they'll go when they die (129).[28]

Ironically, gospel clarity is entirely missing. Even that statement above clouds the gospel truths. What does it mean for people to "open their lives" so they can "be assured" that they will go to Heaven? This would have been a perfect opportunity to "make the way absolutely clear." How does someone go to Heaven? By opening their lives? Is that what the Apostles taught?

The closest thing to a gospel presentation in the whole book is on page 196 where Piper writes:

> Going to heaven that January morning wasn't my choice. The only choice in all of this is that one day I turned to Jesus Christ and accepted him as my Savior. Unworthy as I am, he allowed me to go to heaven, and I know the next time I go there, I'll stay.

That's the closest to a gospel presentation that Piper manages to get. That is pretty pathetic for someone who feels responsible to "make the way absolutely clear." A sinner could not get saved from that presentation even if he wanted to!

There is no presentation of what it is that keeps people out of Heaven (sin). The reader has no idea why he would need Jesus or why he would be excluded from Heaven in the first place. Piper does not talk about sin and our violation of the law of God. He does not speak of God's judgment or the wrath to come, or the need to be born again. Piper does not explain why Jesus died on a cross, what God was doing through that atonement, or the centrality of the resurrection. Piper does not explain that the sinner must **repent** and **trust** in the God-man Jesus Christ alone for salvation or he will face the just wrath of a holy God on Judgment Day.

Piper does say that "we are the reason Jesus Christ wept, suffered, and died on the cross" (107). That mention is not even in the context of talking about sin and the need for salvation, but in the context of recounting how his depression was lifted from him. Piper does not explain why Jesus had to die or why He died for us. In fact, nowhere in the book are we told of any connection between the death of Christ and going to Heaven.

The reader will walk away thinking that salvation comes by "accepting Christ" (196), making a decision or commitment, or opening his life (129). That is not a gospel presentation! He has not made the way absolutely clear.

In spite of his claims that he wants to see people go to Heaven, he has failed in 205 pages to present the message of the gospel which is the power of God unto salvation (Romans 1:16). Unfortunately, many will read his tale of Heaven without ever reading of how to go there.

Criticism #4:
Piper's View of Scripture

I have saved this criticism for last because I believe it is the most pervasive, subtle, unrecognized, and yet destructive error contained in the book. I believe this book undermines the readers' confidence in, encourages distrust of, and excuses unbelief in God's Word. This book elevates experience - specifically his - *above* God's written revelation as a source of comfort, assurance, and hope for the believer and repeatedly suggests that Scripture can be believed because of what Piper has experienced. *I understand that that is a serious charge. Please bear with me. I believe that the following analysis of Piper's teaching will bear this out.*

Piper explains that it took a full two years after the accident before he felt comfortable speaking of his experience with anyone, including his wife (78, 124). He wondered, "How could I put into words that I had had the most joyful, powerful experience of my life?" He felt the experience was "too intimate, too intense to share." It was "too sacred, too special" and wrote, "I felt that talking about my ninety minutes in heaven would defile those precious moments" (78). He writes, "At times I felt that it had been too sacred and that to try to explain it would diminish the incident" (124).

Once he finally opened up, he realized how his experience could serve as a source of hope, encouragement, assurance, and comfort to other Christians.

For instance, when he finally opened up to his friend, David, he became more animated and excited the more Piper shared.

> In retrospect, I believe David's exuberance was a combination of *my personal confirmation of heaven's reality* and his relief in knowing something good had come out of my long nightmare.[29]

He continues to get the same type of reaction from countless people who read his book or hear his talks. He writes:

> I talk about my experience both publicly and to individuals. I'm writing about what happened because my story seems to mean so much to people for many different reasons. For example, when I speak to any large crowd, at least one person will be present who has recently lost a loved one and *needs assurance of that person's destination.* . . . . I feel so grateful that *I can offer*

38

them peace and assurance (128-129).[30]

Do you notice the subtle poison in that statement? If someone needs assurance, why do they need anything more than Scripture? Why is the Bible not enough for the person who needs assurance? It should be. If God has spoken on the issue, why does He need Don Piper to confirm it?

Piper is convinced that because of His experience, he can offer people peace and assurance. He boldly claims:

In fact, my experience has changed many things about the way I look at life. I've changed the way I do funerals. *Now I can speak authoritatively about heaven from firsthand knowledge* (129).[31]

Could Piper not speak authoritatively about Heaven before his experience? Is the only authoritative speaking that which is firsthand? Since I have not made a trip to Heaven (nor has anyone I personally know), am I unable to offer to people peace and assurance or speak authoritatively of its reality? I have some news for Mr. Piper. Any time someone presents what the Bible says and declares the truth of God faithfully, he is speaking with authority on that subject! He doesn't need a trip to Heaven in order to do that. Nor does he need firsthand knowledge. What God has written is more authoritative and certain than his "firsthand knowledge."

During a speaking engagement at First Chinese Baptist Church, Piper offered an explanation for why God would allow him to see Heaven and then send him back to earth.

The question I kept asking more than any is this, "Why did you let me see that and take it away from me?" I thought that was a good question. I have a better answer now in 2008 than I had in 1989 when the big truck hit me. Here it is: So I could stand here today in the First Chinese Baptist

Church and say to you without reservation, "Heaven is real."[32]

That is a stunning tell of Piper's view of the revelation given in Scripture and the authority it carries. Would he be unable to affirm "without hesitation" that Heaven was real if he had never visited it? Is such certainty only available to those who have had an experience like Piper's? Is the revelation of Scripture insufficient to give us that type of confidence and authority on this subject?

This low view of Scripture and high view of his experience is pervasive throughout the book. Piper is convinced that "God brings people into my life who need me or need to hear my message." In a chapter titled "Touching Lives," Piper recounts one very telling episode which took place in a large church where he was invited to speak specifically about his trip to Heaven (157-158). He writes:

> A woman who sat near the front and to my left began to weep shortly after I began to speak. I could see the tears sliding down her cheeks. As soon as we closed the meeting, she rushed up to me and clasped my hand.

> "My mother died last week."

> "I'm so sorry for your loss -"

> "No, no, you don't understand. God sent you here tonight. *I needed this kind of reassurance*. Not that I didn't believe - I did, but my heart has been so heavy because of the loss. I feel so much better. She is in a better place. Oh, Reverend Piper, *I needed to hear that tonight*."

Before I could say anything more, she hugged me and added, "God also sent me here tonight because *I needed this reassurance*. Not that I didn't believe and didn't know - because I'm a believer and so was she - but *I needed to hear those words tonight. I needed to know about heaven from someone who had been there*."

He then adds, "I've heard this kind of response hundreds of times" (157-158).

This woman did not need to hear Piper. She needed to turn to Scripture and hear the Word of God. Despite the many protests to the opposite, this woman was not believing the Bible. She claimed that she needed to hear about Heaven from someone who had been there. What about Jesus? He spoke of Heaven in John 14. He had come from Heaven and had spent far more than ninety minutes there. Not only that, Jesus didn't contradict Himself when talking about it! Is Jesus' testimony not enough? Apparently, for this woman it wasn't. Piper thinks that his words can be of encouragement to those who will not simply trust what Jesus has said.

Consider the case of Charles, a believer who lacked assurance of his salvation and was diagnosed with cancer (170-172). When Sue, Charles's wife, asked Piper to visit Charles and share his experience, Piper did. After four visits, Charles finally started to open up saying, "I'm afraid. I want to go to heaven, but I need assurance - I want to be certain that when I die, I'll go to heaven."

Piper shared some Scripture verses with Charles.

Several times I reminded him of the verses in the Bible that promise heaven as the ultimate destination for all believers.

"I know, I know," he said. "Before I was saved, I

41

knew I wouldn't go to heaven. I was going to hell. Now I want to be sure about heaven."

Stop here in this story for just a moment. Piper did the right thing in giving Him Scripture, but notice Charles's response: "Now I want to be sure about heaven." Does that sound like the response of someone who is believing what the Bible says about Heaven? Is that the response of someone who is taking God at His Word and resting in the truth revealed therein?

Piper continues: "My description of heaven encouraged him. 'Yes, yes, that's what I want,' he said."

What was the source of final encouragement and assurance for Charles? Was it Scripture? Was it Jesus' promises? Was it the Word of God? Was it John's description of Heaven in Revelation 21-22? No. It was Piper's description of Heaven!

Piper continues:

On one visit as he talked, he smiled and said, "I'm ready. I'm at peace. I finally know that I'll go to heaven."

On both of the last two visits I made, Charles said, "Tell me again. Tell me once more what heaven is like."

I told him again, even though he had already heard everything I had to say. It was as if his assurance grew each time I talked about heaven.

Charles's source of assurance was the testimony of Don Piper. Scripture was not enough for Charles. Scripture was not enough for Piper. Piper thinks that his experience is somehow able to do what Scripture cannot - give assurance of Heaven's reality. When Scripture cannot do the trick, you just call Don Piper and he can tell you with true authority from first-hand experience - not all that Bible stuff, but first-hand experience!

Lest you miss the point, Piper boldly states:

Charles's calm assurance and acceptance gave Sue peace as she worked through her own grief and loss. She told me that only weeks before his death, he'd said listening to my experience [*again, not Scripture, but his experience*] and seeing the positive glow in my life [*not Scripture*] made the difference. "It's settled," he'd said. "I know I'm going to a better place."

This is truly sad. To a doubting man, Don Piper gave nothing more than his fallible experience in place of infallible Scripture. Rather than encouraging the man to look to Jesus and His promises, Piper encouraged his doubting of God's written Word by offering his personal experience in its place.

What should Piper have counseled? He should have kept his experience to himself and simply pointed Charles to Jesus' promises. John 5, 6, 10, and 14 would have been good places to start. Piper should have lovingly told Charles that genuine and lasting assurance of Heaven comes not from some man's experience, but from the written Word of the Living God.

One last example comes in the story of Joyce Pentecost (188-190) who died of cancer at the young age of thirty-eight. Piper spoke to her several times before she finally died. Here is one such personal moment he shared during the funeral service:

The last extended conversation I had with Joyce before she returned home from the hospital was about heaven. **She never tired of hearing me**

describe my trip to heaven, so we "visited" there one final time. We talked of the angels, the gate, and our loved ones. . . . Joyce always wanted me to describe the music, and our final conversation together was no different.[33]

It was apparently his experience that gave her hope and prepared her for Heaven, not Scripture. Piper concludes his account of Joyce with this: "Because I was able to experience heaven, I was able to prepare her and her loved ones for it. And now I am preparing you" (190).

Piper claims that he is **uniquely** qualified to address these issues. He claims to be an eyewitness and thus able to speak with authority on the subject (129).

What if he had never visited Heaven? Would he be unable to prepare her and her loved ones for it? Would he be unable to prepare you? What does it say about the rest of us who have never had his experience? Are we unable to prepare people to meet God? Are we unable to speak with authority? Are we ill-equipped to offer assurance since all we have to go on is Scripture?

I believe that Piper betrays his low view of Scripture by subtly suggesting that his experience is at least on par with Scripture or even superior to it. To those who doubt, he offers his experience which he thinks is able to do what Scripture is not, namely, offer assurance, hope, and peace.

Piper is convinced that God brings people into his life who need him or need to hear his message (157). He writes, "For those who already believe, my testimony has been reassuring; for skeptics, it's opened them up to think more seriously about God" (158).

For those who already believe, they don't need his testimony. It contradicts Scripture and is nothing more than one man's alleged experience. That experience is not as reliable as God's written Word (2 Peter 1:16-21), no matter how real he might think it is. Scripture is better. Scripture is sufficient, and the one who takes God at His Word and believes what God has written has no need for Piper or his experience.

Further, his experience cannot cause a skeptic to open up to God or to believe. Jesus said that those who do not believe already have the testimony of Moses and the Prophets and if they are unbelieving, "they will not be persuaded even if someone rises from the dead" (Luke 16:31). Unbelievers are unbelieving not because they lack evidence of Heaven, but because they love darkness. Piper's testimony cannot and will not change that. The subtle assumption behind Piper's words is that his testimony/experience has more power to convince than that of Jesus. What Scripture cannot do, what Jesus cannot do, Piper's testimony can. Piper thinks that his resurrection from the dead can convince the skeptic. Jesus said it can't.

What About YOU, Doubter?

The one who doubts God's Word does not need to be given comfort from an experience which contradicts Scripture. He needs to be reproved for his unbelief! Thousands, I am sure, have read Piper's book trying to get some glimpse into Heaven which Scripture does not afford. Many have read his book hoping to receive some final assurance that Heaven is real. Unwilling to embrace the teaching of Scripture and believe Jesus, they chase after lesser lights - fallible experiences which blatantly contradict Scripture.

That pathetically low view of Scripture and unbelief needs to be confronted and revealed for the sin that it is. If God has written it in His Word, **you do not need Piper to**

45

confirm it. You do not need any to offer their testimony to it's veracity. It is written! To the Word we appeal and we can do no better.

Why would you turn to this book? What are you hoping to glean or gain? Are you hoping to have your faith strengthened? By what, some fallible experience? Are you hoping to read something that confirms Scripture? Why? Is God's Word not enough?

Piper's book appeals to one type of audience - those who refuse to take God solely at His Word and rest soundly in what He has revealed in inspired Scripture. It appeals to those who are looking for something more than Scripture to give them hope, peace, assurance, and confidence that the Bible is true. This is nothing more than rank unbelief and a low view of Scripture masquerading as "faith." As Tim Challies writes:

> Faith is believing that what God says in His Word is true and without error. You dishonor God if you choose to believe what the Bible says only when you receive some kind of outside verification. You dishonor God if you **need** this kind of outside verification.[34]

Readers need to make a choice. Do you believe that Heaven is real? If so, then what forms the basis for your confidence - Scripture or Piper's experience? If Scripture, then Piper's experience is completely unnecessary. Ditch the book. Don't buy it. Don't recommend it. He offers nothing of substance, only confusion and contradiction. If Jesus has spoken, then everything and anything that Don Piper offers is utterly useless. Scripture is enough! Believe it!

What About the Experience?

What should we make of this alleged experience? Piper claims that he visited Heaven for ninety minutes and was sent back here to assure the rest of us that Heaven is real. How do we explain this experience? What can account for it?

The main point of this review is not to try to explain Piper's experience. Just as he feels that his experience does not need to be defended, I feel that his experience does not need to be explained. It is only an experience and I can't exegete it. Nor do I need to be able to offer an alternative explanation for his story. We are under no obligation to believe the word of those who claim to have made trips to Heaven, nor are we even obligated to give them the benefit of the doubt.

However, I believe we can offer a few suggestions that might explain the origin of the story he tells.

1) Piper is lying. That is not a kind thing to suggest, but it is nonetheless a possibility. It is possible that Piper has fabricated this whole experience out of thin air. It is possible that Piper wrote the book for financial gain and found a way to capitalize on a horrible experience. I prefer **not** to believe this about him, but the fact is that we cannot discount this as a real possibility.

2) A Drug-Induced Hallucination. Piper admits in his book that immediately after the accident he was given powerful narcotics and continued to be on some of those drugs for a long period of time. The drugs coupled with the pain would be more than sufficient to explain a bizarre experience, even one as vivid and "real" as this one.

3) A Demonic Deception. Perhaps the experience was not drug-induced but demonically inspired. Piper is not above demonic deception. I have documented enough

47

contradictions between his experience and Scripture to show that whatever Piper experienced, wherever he visited (if he did) was not the Heaven revealed in Scripture. That leaves only one very real possibility - he experienced a very elaborate demonic deception.

Why would demons deceive someone with that type of experience? What if it would lead to pride in the individual and cause him to think of himself as someone special - someone with an experience that can do more than Scripture itself? What if the very retelling of this experience as a source of assurance would serve to confirm people in their unbelief toward God's Word and encourage people to look elsewhere for confirmation and assurance? What if this experience would actually result in people being confused as to the gospel message by a book that does nothing to promote it or make it clear?

I think those things would serve as more than enough motivation for demons to fabricate an experience. Either Piper has been deceived (hallucination or demonically) or he is intentionally deceiving. Either way, this book is poison.

Conclusion

I believe Piper has been deceived, and unfortunately, that deception is embraced by well-meaning Christians. The promotion of his story encourages doubt and unbelief instead of faith and trust. It confuses people about the gospel and encourages people to look away from Scripture for proof of Heaven.

90 Minutes in Heaven presents the joys of Heaven without Jesus, worship in Heaven without the cross, and access to Heaven without the gospel.

I cannot think of one good thing which is accomplished by this book which is not immediately outweighed by its liabilities.

Christian, stay away! There is nothing here worth reading. If you want a true picture of Heaven, read the one given in Revelation and be content with it![35]

Endnotes

1. Baptist General Convention of Texas.

2. Don Piper with Cecil Murphey, *90 Minutes in Heaven: A True Story of Death and Life* (Grand Rapids: Revel, 2004). From this point forward I will simply cite page numbers in parentheses.

3. An ad hominem attack is an attack "against the man" rather than against his argument.

4. Emphasis mine.

5. The Ilizarov bone growth device is an external fixator named after a Siberian doctor (Ilizarov) who invented it. It is used to make bones grow in length (68-69).

6. Stated in an interview aired on ABC's Nightline Television Program. This segment is available in full at http://abcnews.go.com/Nightline/beyondbelief/describing-heaven-pastor-don-piper-pronounced-dead/story?id=14214140#.T9-ZbZHNlIY - time marker 3:05.

7. http://www.challies.com/book-reviews/book-review-90-minutes-in-heaven.

8. See pages 22, 25, 28, 31, 34, 35, and 36.

9. John Piper, *God is the Gospel* (Wheaton: Crossway Books, 2005), 15.

10. Peters' footnote: I do not know these were his exact words but, if not, they are very close. Piper reiterated this claim. . . on May 27, 2011, on TBN's *Praise the Lord* program, . . . : "I began to look up through the gate and I could see this kind of pinnacle in the middle of the city. It's kind of a hill high and lifted up. There's a river flowing down the side of this, well, it's the River of Life and it's coming down the side of this mountain, or hill if you will, and at the top of that is the brightest light I've ever seen and I know Who that is, it's the Lord high and lifted up."

11. You can access Justin Peters' review at http://worldviewweekend.com/worldview-times/article.php?articleid=7575#_ftnref29 . Peters' footnote: For the sake of accuracy, I recorded the audio of this conversation.

12. This was stated in an interview aired on ABC's Nightline Television Program. This segment is available in full at http://abcnews.go.com/Nightline/beyondbelief/describing-heaven-pastor-don-piper-pronounced-dead/story?id=14214140#.T9-ZbZHNlIY - time marker 3:05.

13. All the bold emphasis is mine except Piper's statement, "I can't wait to hear them again - in person," which is emphasized in the original.

14. Scripture references taken from the New American Standard Bible, 1995 Update, unless otherwise noted.

15. Emphasis mine.

16. http://www.youtube.com/watch?v=u8E2UAv_3w4

17. Revelation 5:9-10. Emphasis mine.

18. Revelation 5:11-12. Emphasis mine.

19. Revelation 5:6, 8, 12, 13; 6:1, 7, 9, 16; 7:9, 10, 14, 17; 8:1; 12:11; 13:8, 11; 14:1, 4, 10; 15:3; 17:14; 19:7, 9; 21:9, 14, 22, 23, 27; 22:1, 3.

20. Revelation 5:6; see also Revelation 13:8.

21. You can watch the video at http://www.youtube.com/watch?v=u8E2UAv_3w4. There are no details given about the video as to the date and location, but Piper mentions at about the 51-minute mark that the year was 2008 and that he was speaking at the First Chinese Baptist Church.

22. He says this at the 42:20 time mark and following.

23. Emphasis mine.

24. Piper waited two full years after the accident before telling people of his trip to Heaven (123). He explains this by saying "that it had been too sacred and that to try to explain it would diminish the incident" (124). He explains this delay on pages 78-79 as well.

25. Emphasis mine.

26. Emphasis original.

27. Stated on the back cover of the book.

28. Emphasis mine. During a conversation with Dick Onerecker lamenting their lack of evangelistic zeal Piper relates Dick saying, "Yet here we are sitting in this place, surrounded by people, many of whom are probably lost and going to hell, and we won't say a word about how they can have eternal life. Something is wrong with us."

"You are absolutely right," agreed Piper (130-131).

29. Emphasis mine.

30. Emphasis mine.

31. I hope that he has started presenting the gospel more clearly at funerals than he does in the book or in the few speaking engagements I have watched! Emphasis mine.

32. https://www.youtube.com/watch?v=u8E2UAV_3w4 (Time marker: 50:45-51:33)

33. Emphasis mine.

34. http://www.challies.com/articles/heaven-tourism. Emphasis in original.

35. I would also recommend Randy Alcorn's book, *Heaven* (Tyndale House Publishers). This is not an account of a trip to Heaven, but a biblical, systematic, theological study of all that Scripture reveals about Heaven.

2

A Critical Theological Review of *Heaven Is for Real* by Todd Burpo

Don Piper got it started with his book *90 Minutes in Heaven* which has sold more than 4 million copies in over 22 languages since its publication in 2004.[1] Piper paved the way for the rapid embrace of seemingly credible accounts of trips to Heaven and back. Six years later, in 2010, Christians seemed even more willing to uncritically embrace yet another alleged vision of Heaven, making *Heaven Is for Real*[2] an almost instant best seller. According to available sales figures, *Heaven Is for Real* has sold more than 6 million copies after just two years on the shelf of your local Christian bookstore.

Why This Review

The completely uncritical embrace by the Christian community of any storyteller who wanders by with an account of having visited Heaven is indicative of a lack of discernment among those who name the name of Christ. Sixty years ago, books like this would have never made it off the presses. Any decent publisher would have refused to print such banal nonsense and book stores would never have considered selling such tripe to unsuspecting patrons. Today, it's different.

Claiming to visit Heaven is big business! Just the book sales themselves are worth millions to both author and publisher. Sadly, it seems that nobody is willing to ask the simple question, "Is this true?"

Christians are so desperate to have their theology and faith validated by modern day experiences that they rush to sanction any account which offers authentication. This only serves to undermine the testimony of Scripture and to reveal their own lack of confidence in it.

The Christian church needs discernment. With the proliferation of questionable experiences, we need today, perhaps more than ever, to follow the apostle's injunction to, "examine everything carefully; hold fast to that which is good" (1 Thessalonians 5:21) and to examine the Scriptures daily to see whether these things are so (Acts 17:11).

It is my hope that by exposing error, the hearts of God's people will be turned to the truth of Scripture and they may be equipped to discern the dangers of these alleged modern-day revelations.

Not-So-Critical Reviews

The endorsements inside the book's cover reveal the complete lack of discernment that plagues the modern Christian church.

Don Piper, author of *90 Minutes in Heaven*, tops the list with this unqualified recommendation:

You will be moved by the honest, simple, childlike accounts of a little boy who has been to heaven. It's compelling and convincing. It's a book you should read. If you're ready to go to heaven, this book will inspire you. If you're not ready for heaven, allow a little child to lead you. Like Colton says, Heaven Is for Real.[3]

It is interesting that Piper would endorse an account of a trip to Heaven which contains details that contradict his own. As a pastor, he should have the discernment necessary to identify the horrible false doctrines contained in Colton

52

Burpo's account. Then again, if Piper is skeptical of Colton's account, how can he expect people to uncritically embrace his own? Piper can hardly criticize one account while promoting his own. After all, if God is in the business of offering tours of Heaven, how can we question anyone's claims without questioning everyone's claims?

Equally disturbing is the recommendation offered by Sheila Walsh, author and regular speaker for Women of Faith Conferences:

> Every now and again a manuscript comes across my desk where the title intrigues me. That's what happened with this particular book called *Heaven Is for Real*. I thought I'd just skim through it, but I couldn't put it down. I read it from cover to cover. I was so impacted by the story. It's a book that will not only make you love God more and fear death less, but it will help you understand that heaven is not a place where we just sit around for a thousand years singing Kumbaya; it's a place where we begin to live as we were always meant to live, before the fall. If heaven is something that intrigues you, or troubles you, if you wonder what our lives would be like, then I highly recommend this book.[4]

Sheila Walsh should know better. As a woman who leads and teaches other women, she should have been able to spot the heresies and unbiblical theology presented in this book. Walsh assumes that what is revealed in this book is a genuine revelation of what our lives will be like, a revelation of Heaven that is instructive for us today. She treats Colton's experience as if it were just as true, authoritative, and trustworthy as anything we might find in Scripture. In fact, she points us to this book and not Scripture to learn of Heaven. That is nothing short of tragic!

Among the many other recommendations for this book from senior pastors and presidents of seminaries, is this very telling statement:

> Colton's story could have been in the New Testament - but God has chosen to speak to us in this twenty-first century through the unblemished eyes of a child, revealing some of the mysteries of heaven. The writing is compelling and the truth astonishing, creating a hunger for more.[5]

This highlights one of the fundamental problems with these supposed modern-day visions of Heaven. If the reader accepts them as true, then they are in fact a twenty-first century revelation of Heaven equal in authority to that received by any writer of Scripture. This is an issue I will address a little later in this review.

Summary of the Book

March 2003 brought to the Burpo family a series of harrowing events centering around their then four-year-old son, Colton. Colton, the youngest of their two children[6], suffered from an undiagnosed ruptured appendix while on a family vacation. A series of misdiagnoses and mistreatments allowed his appendix to leak poison into his system for five days. By the time Colton's symptoms were correctly diagnosed, he was very near death.

After Colton's recovery he began to reveal details of his experience as well as things which happened during his surgery. This caused his parents to conclude that Colton had visited Heaven as part of a Near Death Experience while on the operating table.

In "bits and pieces over a period of months and years," Colton began to reveal the details of his "extraordinary journey" (151). Colton's father, Todd,[7] the author of the book,[8] began a process of question-asking and discovery as his son began to reveal the details of his trip to Heaven.

The Process of Discovery

Four months after their harrowing experience in North Platte, Nebraska, the Burpo family, on another trip, was driving past the Great Plains Regional Medical Center where Colton had been treated. Jokingly, Todd Burpo reminded young Colton of the hospital: "Hey, Colton, if we turn here, we can go back to the hospital. Do you wanna go back to the hospital?" (xvii).

Colton answered, "No, Daddy, don't send me!"

Colton's mom, Sonja, asked, "Do you remember the hospital, Colton?"

"Yes, Mommy, I remember," he said. "That's where the angels sang to me."

When asked, "What did they sing to you?" Colton replied, "Well, they sang 'Jesus Loves Me' and 'Joshua Fought the Battle of Jericho.' I asked them to sing, 'We Will, We Will Rock You,' but they wouldn't sing that" (xviii).

During that same conversation, Colton claimed that while in Heaven he sat on Jesus' lap. He then revealed what his parents were doing in the other room while the surgeon was working on him in the operating room. Colton said, "Yeah, at the hospital. When I was with Jesus, you were praying and Mommy was talking on the phone."

Todd responded, "How could you know what we were doing?"

Colton claimed, "'Cause I could see you. I went up out of my body and I was looking down and I could see the doctor working on my body. And I saw you and Mommy. You were in the little room by yourself, praying; and Mommy was in a different room, and she was praying and talking on the phone" (xx).

This was the Burpos' first clue that something extraordinary had happened to their son. From that point, Todd began to question Colton about his experiences to "get him to talking again" (62). He claims he was careful not to ask him leading questions. He didn't want to put any ideas into Colton's head. After all, as Todd says, "If he had really seen Jesus and the angels, I wanted to become the student, not the teacher" (62). How sad is this - a trained and commissioned pastor called to teach the Word making himself the student of a 4-year-old who makes unbiblical claims?

Through the book, Todd continues to relate the conversations he had with Colton, the questions he asked, and the revelations of Heaven that Colton disclosed. Todd even tried on occasion to trick Colton by misleading him with certain suggestions. Once, he suggested that it gets dark in Heaven, only to have Colton correct him. This, Todd believes confirms that Colton really did see Heaven and spend time there.

At no point in the book does Todd question any detail, no matter how ridiculous, that is offered by his son. From the very beginning Todd postured himself as the student and his four-year-old boy as the teacher as he uncritically embraced every detail offered by Colton. Some of the claims are so absurd, unbiblical, and even heretical as to make even the most minimally discerning reader realize that whatever Colton saw, it was not Heaven. But that didn't stop Todd Burpo from lapping it all up without hesitation.

On a number of occasions, we find Todd taking in these silly sophomoric details while describing how he was overwhelmed by the profundity of his child's account. He had to take breaks from all his learning from Colton because, "I had enough information to chew on" (68). After being told that Jesus has a rainbow-colored horse, Todd, not one to be the least bit skeptical, is overwhelmed by the account: "That set my head spinning" (63). On another occasion, Todd's response: "My mind reeled" (66). This is characteristic of the uncritical acceptance given to every detail related by Colton, no matter how bizarre.

At a number of points, Todd, being a pastor, should have discerned that what he was being told by his son did not comport with the biblical description of Heaven. He didn't.

It never seems to occur to him that there could be any explanation for the claims of his imaginative 4-year-old boy other than that he really did visit Heaven. He never entertains the possibility that Colton invented the details. He never considers that Colton might have been deceived. Todd Burpo took it all in without hesitation, question, criticism, or discernment and he apparently expects the reader of this book to do the same.

The Biblical and Theological Problems with Colton's Description of Heaven

Where other accounts are scarce on the actual details concerning their time in Heaven,[9] this book abounds with more than you want. The descriptions of Heaven are nothing like you would find in the book of Revelation. They are, however, exactly the type of details you would expect to be made up by an imaginative 4-year-old.

Claims about Heaven

According to Colton, there are lots of colors in Heaven: "That's where all the rainbow colors are" (63). When asked, "What did you do in heaven?", Colton responded, "Homework." Todd Burpo continues:

> Homework? That wasn't what I was expecting. Choir practice, maybe, but homework? "What do you mean?"
>
> Colton smiled, "Jesus was my teacher."
>
> "Like school?"
>
> Colton nodded. "Jesus gave me work to do, and that was my favorite part of heaven. There were lots of kids, Dad" (71-72).

We are supposed to believe that Jesus is busy teaching children in Heaven and assigning homework! These are the kinds of inane and immature details that litter the landscape of this book. This is not something we find in Scripture, but it is something we would expect a four-year-old to fabricate. Why do we not read of details like this in the lengthy and inspired account of the book of Revelation? Perhaps it is because Colton's description of Heaven does not fit reality.

When asked whether Colton saw any animals in Heaven, Todd writes, "The answer is yes! Besides Jesus' horse, he told us he saw dogs, birds, even a lion - and the lion was friendly, not fierce" (152).

Catholics are curious about Heaven as well.

> A lot of our Catholic friends have asked whether Colton saw Mary, the mother of Jesus. The answer

to that is also yes. He saw Mary kneeling before the throne of God and at other times standing beside Jesus. "She still loves him like a mom," Colton said (152-153).

Colton would only say this because he is too young and immature to understand that Mary, in Heaven, loves Christ, not like a mom, but like a sinner saved by grace.

Wings

After Colton revealed that "there were lots of kids" in Heaven, Todd Burpo writes, "But all I could think to ask was: 'So what did the kids look like? What do people look like in heaven?'"

"Everybody's got wings," Colton said.

Wings, huh?

"Did you have wings?" I asked.

"Yeah, but mine weren't very big." He looked a little glum when he said this.

"Okay . . . did you walk places or did you fly?"

"We flew. Well, all except for Jesus. He was the only one in heaven who didn't have wings. Jesus went up and down like an elevator" (72).

Todd Burpo then lamely tries to liken that juvenile description to the Ascension of Christ in Acts 1, as if the Ascension had anything at all to teach about Jesus' mode of movement in Heaven.

Colton then revealed, "Everyone kind of looks like angels in heaven, Dad. . . . All the people have a light above their head" (73).

Later, Colton described seeing his grandfather, Todd's father, whom he calls Pop. Todd asked, "Colton, what did Pop look like?"

"He broke into a big grin. 'Oh, Dad, Pop has really big wings!'" (87).

Of course, Scripture does not teach that those in Heaven have wings and need them to move. This should have caused skepticism in anyone with even a minimal level of discernment and knowledge of the Bible.

The ghost writer of this book, Lynn Vincent, was reluctant to include this detail expecting that it would be a sure signal to Bible-believing Christians that the Burpo account was fraudulent. She admits, "If I put that people in Heaven have wings, orthodox Christians are going to think that the book is a hoax."[10] She included it in the account, and millions of undiscerning Christians swallowed it without question. She apparently thought far more highly of the discernment skills of Christians than is warranted.

This account contradicts Don Piper's *90 Minutes in Heaven*. In his book, Piper claims that he saw a crowd of people at Heaven's gate, all sent to welcome him, yet he doesn't mention that any of them had wings. According to Piper, he started walking toward Heaven's gate, not flying:

Strange as it seems, as brilliant as everything was, each time I **stepped forward**, the splendor increased. The farther I **walked**, the brighter the light. . . . A holy awe came over me as I **stepped forward**. I had no idea what lay ahead, but I sensed that with **each step I took**, it would grow more wondrous.[11]

In fact, Piper says that he felt that those who greeted him "wanted to walk beside me as I passed through the iridescent gate."[12]

Remember, Piper endorses this book even though reports like this one undermine his own claims. Why does Piper not mention this detail? Does he concur with Burpo's claim that people in Heaven have wings and move by flying? If not, then why does he endorse something he knows to be false? If he does, then why does his own account offer different details? One of these persons is lying.

The Throne of God

Colton claims that he saw God's throne "a bunch of times" (100). He said Jesus was next to God's throne. When asked what side of the Father Jesus sat on, Colton confirmed it was the right side (101).

Todd writes:

Wow. Here was a rare case where I had tested Colton's memories against what the Bible says, and he passed without batting an eye. But now I had another question, one I didn't know the answer to, at least not an answer from the Bible.[13]

"Well, who sits on the other side of God's throne?" I said.

"Oh, that's easy, Dad. That's where the angel Gabriel is. He's really nice" (101).

Todd Bupro was asking for information about Heaven that he admitted was not to be found in Scripture. I wonder if we are to start writing some of this down as an appendix in our Bibles. We know Jesus sits at the right hand of the Father. We are told that by the inspired author of Hebrews. Now, equally authoritative I guess, we are to know that Gabriel sits at God's left hand.

Colton further claims that he got to sit down in God's throne room. Todd asked him, "Where did you sit, Colton?"

He replied:

"They brought in a little chair for me. . . I sat by God the Holy Spirit. . . . I was sitting by God the Holy Spirit because I was praying for you. You needed the Holy Spirit, so I prayed for you" (102).

Why would anyone who has read the descriptions of God's presence in Isaiah, Ezekiel, or Revelation give this even one moment's consideration? This is not the picture that the Bible paints for us. It is, however what we might expect from the fertile imagination of a four-year-old boy.

Claims about Jesus

During Colton's alleged visit to Heaven he claims that he got to see Jesus. In fact, Colton assured a dying man that, "It's going to be okay. The first person you're going to see is Jesus" (119).[14] Colton not only claims to have seen Jesus, but he has offered plenty of details about the Jesus he saw.

For instance, Colton says he sat on Jesus' lap (xix), Jesus has a horse that is rainbow-colored, and Colton got to pet it (63). This horse must be a different one than the one John saw in his revelation of Heaven (Revelation 6:2; 19:11, 14). Colton relates that Jesus has a beard, His eyes are "pretty," and Jesus wears a purple sash. In fact, He is the only one in Heaven who wears a purple sash (65). Jesus wears a crown with a diamond in the middle (65-66) and the wounds of the cross are still visible. Colton describes the wounds as red "markers" on Jesus.

Claims about the Holy Spirit

It is hard to select the most absurdly laughable and inane detail of the book, but Colton's description of the Holy Spirit would certainly rank in the top five.

Todd asked Colton, "What does God look like? God the Holy Spirit?"

"Colton furrowed his brow. 'Hmm, that's kind of a hard one. . . he's kind of blue" (103).

The Holy Spirit is blue? Blue? Is He a blue fog? A blue person? A blue cloud? Does He look like a smurf? You certainly won't find that in the Bible! And rather than allowing such silly, unbiblical ideas to cause him to question Colton's tale, Todd uncritically received it and tried to picture it in his mind.

Extra-Biblical Revelation

Nobody who believes that the Bible is completely sufficient for the believer would write a book like *Heaven Is for Real*. The very premise of this book is to reveal things about Heaven that we do not or cannot learn from Scripture. Further, we are expected to take the word of a 4-year-old boy for this revelation. It should not surprise us to find out Todd Burpo believes God speaks outside of Scripture to His people to reveal His will for their lives.

Personal Direction

He writes:

Then Mom asked Colton an odd question. "Did Jesus say anything about your dad becoming a pastor?"

"Oh, yes! Jesus said he went to Daddy and told him he wanted Daddy to be a pastor and Daddy said yes, and Jesus was really happy" (90-91).

Todd then describes the night that this happened which he remembered so well. While thirteen, he attended a summer camp at John Brown University in Siloam Springs, Arkansas. After one of the messages which encouraged the kids to pursue being pastors and missionaries, Todd says:

I remember that the crowd of kids faded away and

the reverend's voice receded into the background. I felt a pressure in my heart, almost a whisper: *That's you, Todd. That's what I want you to do.*

There was no doubt in my mind that I had just heard from God (91).

The teaching that God reveals His will apart from Scripture is a denial of Sola Scriptura. Todd Burpo believes that he received personalized, private revelation from God, apart from Scripture. It is no wonder he would believe that he could also receive revelation about Heaven and the future from a 4-year-old's visit to Heaven. This undermines the doctrine of the authority and sufficiency of Scripture.

The Future - Armageddon

Not only did Jesus reveal His will to Todd through personal revelation, but Jesus supposedly revealed the future to Todd through little Colton Burpo. Supposedly Colton got to witness the battle of Armageddon while in Heaven. He got a preview of events to come.

Colton said:

"Dad, did you know there's going to be a war?"

"What do you mean?" Were we still on the heaven topic? I wasn't sure.

"There's going to be a war, and it's going to destroy this world. Jesus and the angels and the good people are going to fight against Satan and the monsters and the bad people. I saw it. . . . In heaven, the women and the children got to stand back and watch. So I stood back and watched. . . . But the men, they had to fight. And Dad, I watched you. You have to fight too."

64

Todd needed clarification.

"You said we're fighting monsters?"

"Yeah," Colton said happily. "Like dragons and stuff."

"Um, Colton . . . what am I fighting the monsters with?" I was hoping for a tank, maybe, or a missile launcher. . . I didn't know, but something I could use to fight from a distance.

Colton looked at me and smiled. "You either get a sword or a bow and arrow, but I don't remember which."

Colton was describing the battle of Armageddon and saying I was going to fight in it (136-138).[15]

Todd believes that he received this private, personalized revelation not available in Scripture. He assumes that this type of revelation is still being given today, that it is reliable, and authoritative. Can you see how this undermines a belief in the sufficiency of Scripture?

Any Christian who believes seriously that Scripture is sufficient would immediately reject such nonsense. Todd did not. He received it without a hint of skepticism, as do many other Christians.

Babies in Heaven - Mystery Solved!

Another example of their view of this extra-Biblical revelation is seen in how they responded when Colton revealed that he had met his sister in Heaven, a sister who tragically miscarried before Colton was even born.

Allegedly, one day, quite out of the blue, Colton quipped, "Mommy, I have two sisters." When questioned, he continued, "I have two sisters. You had a baby die in your tummy, didn't you?"

Colton's mom asked, "Who told you I had a baby die in my tummy?"

Colton replied, "She did, Mommy. She said she died in your tummy" (94).

Colton even described her as "a little bit smaller" than his older sister with dark hair (95).

Colton claimed that, while in Heaven, a little girl ran up to him and wouldn't stop hugging him. He further revealed that this little girl did not have a name since Todd and Sonja had not named their miscarried child. They had not known whether it was a boy or a girl. They insist that Colton could not have known these details.

Their response? After Colton left the room, tears spilled over her cheeks and she said, "Our baby is okay. Our baby is okay" (96).

Then Todd Burpo writes:

We had wanted to believe that our unborn child had gone to heaven. Even though the Bible is largely silent on this point, we had accepted it on faith. But now, we had an eyewitness: a daughter we had never met was waiting eagerly for us in eternity (97).

First, the Bible is not largely silent on this point. There is plenty of evidence that babies go to Heaven when they die.[16]

Second, notice how this revelation from Colton is accepted as an authoritative eyewitness account which gives us information that the Bible does not offer - at least from Todd Burpo's view.

Burpo is asserting that where the Bible is silent, his son can speak with authority. If you have wondered what happens to babies when they die, you can wonder no more. He can tell you. Colton is an eyewitness who has settled the dispute for us. No longer do we have to study Scripture to find out. No longer do we have to take it by faith since "the Bible is largely silent." But the *Burpos* can tell us and we can fix our hope on that.

Todd Burpo is claiming that something was revealed to his boy that was not revealed to the prophets and apostles. Most tragically, Burpo's confidence in the eternal destiny of his unborn child rests, not on Scripture, but on the testimony of his four-year-old boy! The *Bible* offered him no certainty, but now he has assurance because of Colton's *experience*. This speaks volumes about the Burpos' view of Scripture and personal experience.

I hope you can see the hubris inherent in such a view. According to Burpo, information on such an emotional and important topic was not revealed by God to His people until Colton Burpo came along and had his experience. Are we to conclude that this is because God's Word is inadequate? Or was God just negligent? Was this an oversight? Whatever the reason for this lack of revelation, God has supposedly remedied it by giving us the Burpo experience.

You see, until now, until Colton Burpo, our understanding was limited, flawed, and inadequate. But now, thanks to Todd and Colton Burpo, we can know the things about Heaven and God's plan that millions of Christians before us did not know. All they had to go on was the Bible, but we have The Bible plus *Heaven Is for Real*. Aren't you thankful?

Miscellaneous Theological Concerns

As if all of the above were not sufficient reason for rejecting this book as a blasphemous assault on Scripture, there are a number of other theological concerns with the book.

The Plan of Redemption

Reflecting on his love for his son and his anguish during their trial, Todd Burpo offers this nugget of insight:

> The Scripture says that as Jesus gave up his spirit, as he sagged there, lifeless on that Roman cross, God the Father turned his back. I am convinced that he did that because if he had kept on watching, **he couldn't have gone through with it** (149).[17]

The Bible does not say that the Father turned His back on the Son while the Son was on the cross. Burpo's speculation as to the reason is equally spurious: because the Father could not bear to watch what was happening to His Son. Does Burpo really believe that the Father was somehow shielded from the reality of the cross, or guarded from it's harshness because He "turned away" and so He wasn't looking on it? Does God not know about things that He cannot see? Is there anything that God cannot see?

Further, to suggest that the plan of redemption purposed by the Triune God for His eternal glory, somehow hinged upon the flaky emotional state of the Father and His weak stomach for pain and suffering is nothing short of blasphemous!

The cross was God's predetermined plan to accomplish the redemption of sinners for His own eternal glory (Acts 2:22-24, 4:28; John 6:35-44). The Father planned redemption and sent the Son to accomplish it. Are we to think that the Father's plan and the Son's ability to fulfill that plan and save God's elect hung in the balance and was nearly derailed by the Father's vacillating willingness to "go through with it"?

Does Burpo think that the Father did not know what this plan of redemption would cost? Is the Father's plan so fickle that He can be deterred by the prospect of pain? Does he believe that the eternally decreed plan of redemption for God's elect is that uncertain? Apparently, he does.

Power in Preaching

If you think that Colton's visions of the supernatural stopped with his out-of-body experiences, you would be wrong. The Burpos claim that Colton is still able to witness things happening in the spiritual realm.

One evening, as Sonja was putting Colton to bed, she suggested that they pray for his father, Todd, to have a good message in church on Sunday morning. Colton looked at her and said, "I've seen power shot down to Daddy."

"What do you mean, Colton?"

"Jesus shoots down power for Daddy when he's talking."

Sonya asked, "Okay. . . when? Like when Daddy talks at church?"

Colton nodded. "Yeah, at church. When he's telling Bible stories to people" (125).

Not one to critically question *anything* that might come from a four-year-old, Todd Burpo waited until the next morning to quiz Colton. Todd writes:

"Hey, buddy," I said, pouring milk into Colton's usual bowl of cereal. "Mommy said you were talking last night during Bible story time. Can you tell me what you are telling mommy about . . . About Jesus shooting down power? What's the power like?"

"It's the Holy Spirit," Colton said simply. "I watched him. He showed me."

"The Holy Spirit?"

"Yeah, he shoots down power for you when you're talking in church" (125-126).

So not only does Colton have the ability to visit Heaven and report to us infallible details of the life to come, but he is also able to see the secret and supernatural workings of the Holy Spirit. Does Todd Burpo question any of this? Does he seem the least bit skeptical? No. He responds with nothing but an uncritical embrace of anything his four-year-old tells him.

Why should I believe that a likely unregenerated four-year-old boy is privy to the secret and supernatural workings of the Holy Spirit?

A Picture of Jesus

Todd claims that over the course of the months following Colton's alleged visit to Heaven, they discussed what Jesus looked like. Whenever they would see a portrait or painting of Jesus hanging in a hospital, church, or Christian bookstore, they would ask Colton if the picture was a good portrayal of Jesus as he saw Him in Heaven. They would ask him, "What about this one? Is that what Jesus looks like?" (93).

According to Burpo:

Invariably, Colton would peer for a moment at the picture and shake his tiny head. "No, the hair's not right," he would say. Or, "The clothes aren't right."

This would happen dozens of times over the next

three years. Whether it was a poster in a Sunday school room, a rendering of Christ on a book cover, or a reprint of an old Masters painting hanging on the wall of an old folks home, Colton's reaction was always the same: he was too young to articulate exactly what was wrong with every picture; he just knew they weren't right (93-94).

Supposedly, this happens so frequently that it had gotten to the point where instead of asking him, "Is this one right?" they had started asking, right off the bat, "So what's wrong with this one?" (115).

Finally, three years after Colton's alleged visit to Heaven, Todd Burpo was exposed to a December 2006 CNN story about a young Lithuanian-American girl named Akiane Kramarik who lives in Idaho.[18] According to the CNN documentary available at her website, she began painting at the age of six. However, at the age of four, she began to describe to her mother her visits to Heaven. This little girl began to tell her stories of Heaven and then to depict them in her drawings and paintings.

Todd Burpo found an online picture of her painting titled "Prince of Peace" and called Colton into the room. Burpo writes, "Still, of the literally dozens of portraits of Jesus we'd seen since 2003, Colton had still never seen one he thought was right" (144).

Until he saw the portrait painted by the little girl who also visited Heaven. "Take a look at this. What's wrong with this one?" Todd asked.

He turned to the screen and for a long moment said nothing.

"Colton?"

But he just stood there, studying. I couldn't read

his expression.

After a bit, Colton claimed, "Dad, that one's right"(145).

Todd Burpo claims that Colton hadn't known the portrait, called *Prince of Peace: The Resurrection*, was painted by another child - a child who had also claimed to visit Heaven.

For Todd, this was proof positive that, not only had his boy visited Heaven and seen Jesus, but so had another girl who had perfectly captured the Jesus she saw in a painting. For me, this just simply proves that two 4-year-olds were both deceived by the same demon.

If Todd Burpo is right, if this is the Jesus of Heaven, then every other portrait of Jesus should be scrapped and Aikane's picture should come standard in every Bible printed. If this is the real Jesus, then we have an eyewitness to Jesus' physical features. Details not contained in Scripture have been captured on canvas for us. What God kept apostles and prophets from revealing, He has now revealed to us through a couple of children who visited Heaven when they were four. We wonder no longer what Jesus looks like in His glorified state. We can now place alongside inspired writings, an inspired portrait of Jesus from an eyewitness.

Can you see where this nonsense leads us?

Gospel Presentation

One feature that relentlessly plagues these accounts of alleged trips to Heaven is the complete lack of gospel presentation. Neither Don Piper's book nor the Burpo book contain anything that approaches a clear understanding and communication of essential gospel truths.

Todd seems to think that Colton had a sufficient grasp of the essential doctrines of the gospel when he (Colton) asked about a deceased man at his funeral, "Did the man have Jesus in his heart?" (57-58). Colton insisted, "He had to have Jesus in his heart! He had to know Jesus or he can't get into Heaven!"

Of course, one must know Jesus Christ savingly. Without a saving relationship to Christ as Lord and Savior through repentance and faith in His death and resurrection on our behalf, we cannot get into Heaven. Todd Burpo never shares this vital information. He reminds us that Jesus loves children, that Jesus loves everyone, and that Heaven is real. However, there is no presentation of the gospel which might bring someone to a saving knowledge of Christ.

This book contains no presentation of the law of God, sin, the wrath of God, the reality of or reason for Hell, the justice of God, or even the reason that Jesus died on a cross. We are told that Jesus died, but how that applies to lost sinners is never explained. Further, there is no mention of the need for repentance or personal faith in Christ as the satisfaction for God's wrath.

Todd Burpo's understanding of the gospel is seen in a conversation with Colton that he records.

"Colton, do you know why Jesus died on the cross?"

He nodded, surprising me a bit.

"Okay, why?"

"Well, Jesus told me he died on the cross so we could go see his Dad" (111).

Understandably, this is the language employed by a five-year-old (at the time). We could allow for some lack of

73

clarity and precision from Colton, but it is what Todd says next that is truly sad: "Colton's answer to my question was the simplest and sweetest declaration of the gospel I had ever heard" (111).

Has Todd Burpo never read 1 Corinthians 15:3-4? *Paul gives the simplest and sweetest declaration of the gospel I have ever heard!* Colton's answer does not tell us that Jesus died to atone for sin, to pay a sin price. It does not tell us why His death was necessary or how one comes to Heaven because of it. Do we all get to go to Heaven? Does everyone go? How is His death applied to me? How do I get to Heaven through that? Those questions are never answered by this, the "simplest and sweetest declaration of the gospel" that Todd Burpo has ever heard.

Why is the gospel missing in this book? If Heaven is real and Hell is real, and if Todd Burpo is so absolutely convinced of these verities, then why would he withhold or leave out the most valuable detail imaginable, namely, the message of the gospel that rescues people from Hell and takes them to Heaven?

If God were going to be in the business of revealing His Heaven to living visionaries today, don't you think He would choose someone of sound doctrine who would actually understand and communicate the gospel message? Why is it that those who visit Heaven always demonstrate such horrible theological confusion and ignorance of the gospel? Maybe it is not God who is the source of these experiences after all.

Scripture Twisting

Todd Burpo's use of Scripture in this book is nothing short of perverse. Whenever a word, a phrase, or an image from Scripture can be somehow employed to reflect a similarity to something communicated by Colton, Todd

74

does not hesitate to reference it. Todd Burpo abuses the Word of God in order to lend credibility to Colton's experience. Consider the following examples.

Acts 1

On page 72-73, Colton claimed that Jesus was the only one in Heaven without wings. "Jesus just went up and down like an elevator." Then Todd Burpo writes:

> The book of Acts flashed into my head, the scene of Jesus' ascension,. . . Jesus went up. And will come down. Without wings. To a kid, that could look like an elevator (72-73).

Is that what the account in Acts is intended by Luke to tell us - the mode of Jesus' transportation in Heaven? Luke was describing how Jesus ascended from Earth to Heaven in the presence of His disciples. Colton was describing how Jesus gets around in the current Heaven. Yet we are supposed to think that Acts 1 lends credibility to Colton's account just because, in both instances, Jesus ascends. This supposedly makes Colton's claim that everyone has wings sound biblical. That is an abuse of the text that would make a Jehovah's Witness blush! If only it stopped there.

2 Peter 3:8

When Colton claimed that his time in Heaven had only lasted three minutes, Todd tried to figure out how Colton could have met everybody he claimed to have met and done all the things he claimed to have done in only three minutes of time. He finally concluded:

> It was also possible that time in heaven doesn't track with time on earth. The Bible says that with the Lord, a day is like a thousand years, and a thousand years are like a day (2 Peter 3:8) (78).

This verse has nothing to do with the perception or keeping of time in Heaven. Peter is reminding his readers that, though from our perspective, we may get anxious waiting for the promises of God to be fulfilled, God works on His own timetable. God is not late in fulfilling His purposes, but right on time since God is not affected by time the way we are. Burpo uses this verse as if it is intended to show us that time passes in Heaven differently than on earth. It is not describing time in Heaven at all!

Luke 1:19

When Colton revealed that Gabriel sits on God's left hand, Todd found a verse that "proves" that as well.

Gabriel. That makes sense. I remembered the story of John the Baptist and the moment when Gabriel arrived to deliver the news of John the Baptist's coming birth (101).

He then quotes Luke 1:19: "The angel answered and said to him, 'I am Gabriel, who stands in the presence of God, . . . '" (102).

This is offered as proof of Colton's claim, "And now, more than two thousand years later, my little boy was telling me the same thing" (102).

Actually, no. His boy was claiming that Gabriel sits on the left hand of the throne of the Father the way that Jesus sits on His right. That is not something described in Luke's account. Gabriel claimed that he "stands" in God's presence. Colton claims that Gabriel sits at the left hand of God's throne.

But, for Todd Burpo, that is enough biblical support for Colton's extra-biblical revelation. The Bible mentions Gabriel being in God's presence, therefore we should trust Colton's outlandish claims! Never mind the details!

Hebrews 12:1

Colton claims that he was able to know of his parents' need for the Holy Spirit while in Heaven and so, while there, he was praying for them (102). This reminded Todd of another passage of Scripture he could twist.

> This took my breath away. Colton saying that he was praying for me in heaven reminded me of the letter to the Hebrews, where the writer says: "Therefore, since we are surrounded by such a great cloud of witnesses. . . . let us run with perseverance the race marked out for us" (Hebrews 12:1) (102).

In Hebrews 12:1, the "great cloud of witnesses" is a reference to the extended list of saints given in chapter 11 who accomplished great things by faith. These men and women are examples to us of living a life of faith in a hostile world, trusting in the promises of God to His people. What does this have to do with Colton's ability to know of his parents' plight back on Earth? Todd does not explain, so we are left to conjecture what connection Todd Burpo saw between the Hebrews passage and his son's claims. It seems that Todd is referring to Colton's claim to have "witnessed" His parents' need from Heaven. Can you see the connection? Hebrews speaks of dead people being witnesses to us. Colton witnessed us back on Earth. See? See?! See how biblical Colton's statements are?

Hebrews 12:1 is not saying that these "witnesses" are in Heaven watching us, but rather that they give testimony; they give witness to us that the life of faith is duly rewarded. But, for Todd Burpo, all that is needed to press a text of Scripture into service to support his son's outlandish claims is some conceptual connection, even if that connection is only apparent to Todd. No stretch is too much. The intended meaning of the passage never stands in the way of Todd using it to lend credibility to his son's claims.

Mark 10:14

Todd Burpo uses Jesus' statement in Mark 10:14 to validate the supposed heavenly visitations and visions of Akiane Kramarik, "Permit the children to come to Me. . . ."

This is quoted to show that "God can reach anyone, anywhere, at any age - even a preschool girl in a home where his name had never been spoken" (143).

Supposedly, this little girl started visiting Heaven when she was only four years old and then began to report what she saw. Her mother, who had been an atheist, slowly "began to accept that Akiane's visions were real and that therefore, God must be real" (143). All of this is supposedly what Jesus meant when He said, "Let the little children come to me."

In the context of Mark 10:14, Jesus uses the simple trust of a child to illustrate the faith that is necessary to enter the Kingdom. The dependence of a child upon the will and goodness of others for their provision is what is commended. Jesus was saying that the person who imagines that he or she is somehow worthy of God's favor or that their entrance into the kingdom is somehow merited by social rank, will never see the Kingdom. They must come like a child, recognizing they have nothing, completely dependent upon the will and work of God on their behalf. The application of this is seen in the very next passage (Mark 10:17-31) where Jesus encounters the Rich Young Ruler.

But to Todd Burpo, this statement was proof that God is in the business of revealing Himself to theologically unsound four-year-olds.

2 Corinthians 12:1-6

Todd Burpo's use of this passage is an example of both ignorance of Scripture and misuse of Scripture. He cites Paul's vision of Heaven mentioned in 2 Corinthians 12, but misses a very important detail, namely, that the person Paul is describing in the third person is himself. Burpo writes:

Then I remembered that the Bible talks in several places about people who had seen heaven without dying. The apostle Paul wrote to the church at Corinth about a Christian he new personally who was taken to heaven, "Whether it was in the body or out of the body I do not know - God knows. And I know that this man. . . was caught up to paradise. He heard inexpressible things, things that man is not permitted to tell" (80).

Burpo should know better! Though the apostle Paul is speaking in the third person, he is describing himself, which is evident from verse 7:

Because of the surpassing greatness of the revelations, for this reason, to keep **me** from exalting **myself**, there was given **me** a thorn in the flesh, a messenger of Satan to torment **me** - to keep **me** from exalting **myself** (emphasis mine).

Who was this man that went to Heaven and received such a spectacular revelation? It was Paul, not some Christian he personally knew. Is Todd Burpo really that ignorant of Scripture?

Not only does he show ignorance of this passage, which he supposedly knew so well that it popped into his mind during a conversation with Colton (80), but he misuses the passage as well. He cites this passage[19] as proof that people can visit Heaven without dying.

Todd had always believed that people had to die to visit Heaven, yet when he read the Operative Report,[20] he noticed there was no mention of Colton dying on the operating table. He tried to square this with what he reads (or better, misreads) in Scripture. That is when he realized that the Bible gives accounts of people seeing Heaven without dying. Burpo uses the account of Paul's revelation as proof that his son could go to Heaven without suffering physical death.

It does not follow that since revelations were given to inspired apostles hand-picked by Christ for the writing of the New Testament, God is therefore giving similar and even more detailed revelations to 4-year-olds today. This should be obvious to any student of Scripture.

The desire that Burpo has to prove the legitimacy of his son's experience may be what caused him to get the details of Paul's revelation wrong. After all, if it was the Apostle Paul that had the revelation, then Burpo would certainly be hard-pressed to suggest this is normative. It would be even more difficult to prove it so. However, if it was just someone Paul knew - another average Christian - then that certainly suggests that this type of thing was common in the early church. If common then, the reasoning goes, it would be more likely now. The way in which Burpo gets that detail wrong is, at least, suggestive that it is experience that drives his understanding of Scripture and not the other way around.

Further, Burpo's citation of Paul actually proves fatal to his own claims. It is a bit ironic that Burpo quotes the part of the passage where Paul says he is not permitted to reveal what he saw. Paul said he "was caught up into Paradise and heard inexpressible words, which a man is not permitted to speak" (2 Corinthians 12:4).[21]

Paul saw and heard things he was not permitted to describe. If Paul wasn't permitted, why is Colton? The very passage that Burpo cites to show that his son could visit Heaven teaches that if he had, he wouldn't be permitted to speak of it! Yet this entire book is just that: accounts of Colton speaking of Heaven!

And what are we to make of the fact that Paul, a great, mature, godly man, had to be given an affliction to keep him humble after such a revelation? What about Colton? Does he not have any pride? Are we to believe that there was danger of Paul falling into the sin of pride, but there is no danger of that for Colton or Todd? A mature apostle is not permitted to speak of his time in Heaven, but a four-year-old boy can. A godly, seasoned apostle is afflicted to keep him humble, but a four-year-old boy who can't even clearly articulate the gospel needs no such safe-guard.

You should be able to spot the hubris, and it is not in Paul.

Revelation 21:23

At one point Todd tried to trick Colton into saying something about Heaven which might be wrong. He said to Colton:

"I remember you saying you stayed with Pop. So when it got dark and you went home with Pop, what did you two do?"

Suddenly serious, Colton scowled at me. "It doesn't get dark in heaven, Dad! Who told you *that*?"

I held my ground. "What do you mean it doesn't get dark?"

"God and Jesus light up heaven. It never gets

dark. It's always bright."

The joke was on me. Not only had Colton not fallen for the "when it gets dark in heaven" trick, but he could tell me why it didn't get dark: "The city does not need the sun or the moon to shine on it, for the glory of God gives it light, and the Lamb is its lamp" (104).

Burpo is quoting from Revelation 21:23. Strictly speaking, this verse does not refer to the present Heaven, but to the future Heaven: the New Heaven and Earth. In that passage, John is describing the New Jerusalem in the future, eternal Heaven. Burpo cites the passage as if it were describing the present Heaven and thus fitting Colton's description.

Granted, this is not a huge error, but it is another example of Todd Burpo using a passage without regard to its context or meaning.

This type of serial abuse of Scripture is inexcusable! Todd's misuse of biblical texts demonstrates an ignorance of their context, theology, and basic principles of interpretation. Todd Burpo is a pastor, and as one who believes himself called to lead and teach others, he should be able to evidence some ability to exegete Scripture and interpret it properly. Unfortunately for Todd, those he leads, and those who read this book, he lacks that ability.

Conclusion

The popularity of this book is itself a sad commentary on the state of modern evangelicalism. It is evidence that the church is suffering from a lack of discernment and concern for the truth. Todd Burpo demonstrates a complete lack of critical thinking ability and biblical discernment.

This book only serves to undermine confidence in the sufficiency, authority, and truth of Scripture. Christians are asked to base their confidence in Scripture's teaching upon the unreliable and unconfirmed testimony of a small child. Colton's claims do not present a picture of Heaven that is consistent with Scripture (Todd Burpo's abuse of Scripture to make it appear so, not withstanding). This book consistently twists, misrepresents, and wrongly applies God's Word.

This book is poison to the Body of Christ. Some will mistakenly think that they can "eat the meat and spit out the bones." This book is all bones. There is nothing redeeming in this book. Its blasphemies, abuse of Scripture, and childish portrayal of God make this book fit only for the trash heap. Its portrayal of the gospel is tragic. Its description of Heaven childish. Its theology is a train wreck. Its effect can only be ruinous by any measure.

Why would God give a revelation of Heaven to a four-year-old boy whose ability to communicate is limited not only by his age, but his theologically undiscerning father? Why is this visit to Heaven riddled with contradictions to Scripture? Why is this account such a theological wreck? Let the discerning reader ask, "Can this really be the work of God?" I believe the clear answer is no.

Heaven is real. I believe this not because I personally know anyone who claims to have gone there. It is not because I have read the accounts of Colton Burpo or Don Piper. It is because Jesus says so. God's Word is clear enough and it is sufficient. I believe it. I don't need Colton Burpo to confirm it. In fact, I don't need anyone to give me confirmation. I am as certain about the reality of Heaven as I am of my own existence.

The Word of God makes books like *Heaven Is for Real* completely unnecessary. Scripture tells us everything we need to know about Heaven. It tells us everything God wants us to know about Heaven. If God had intended more, He would have included it from the inspired writers of Scripture. Rest in Scripture and Scripture alone. May this book and all of its details be quickly forgotten and lost to the dustbin of history.

Endnotes

1. Sales figure taken from http://www.challies.com/articles/heaven-tourism.
2. Todd Burpo, *Heaven Is for Real* (Dallas: Thomas Nelson, 2010).
3. Inside cover.
4. Inside cover.
5. Inside cover. This comes from Jo Anne Lyon, General Superintendent of The Wesleyan Church.
6. Colton has one sister two years older than he and the Burpos had lost one child in a miscarriage before Colton was even born. This is a detail that Colton supposedly learned during his time in Heaven.
7. Todd Burpo is the pastor of Crossroads Wesleyan Church in Imperial, Nebraska.
8. The book is co-authored by Lynn Vincent who worked for eleven years as senior writer, then features editor at the national news biweekly *WORLD Magazine*. She is currently a lecturer in writing at the World Journalism Institute and at the The King's College in New York City. Frankly, I would have expected more discernment from someone who wrote for *WORLD Magazine* for eleven years. I don't understand how someone who teaches journalism can accept this story with all it's contradictions to Scripture so uncritically. It is unfortunate that someone who cannot even vet this story sufficiently would be teaching future journalists.
9. Don Piper's book *90 Minutes in Heaven* spends only 15 of its 205 pages discussing his time in Heaven, and even those 15 pages offer scant detail.
10. http://www.nypost.com/p/news/opinion/opedcolum nists/csi_afterlife_YLOGrr04p9zP8bShR9QuiN
11. Don Piper, *90 Minutes in Heaven* (Grand Rapids: Fleming H. Revel, 2004), 28. Emphasis mine.
12. Ibid., 35. In spite of all his language which describes him as "stepping" in Heaven, Piper, when asked, "How did you move? Did you walk? Did you float?" has to confess, "I don't know" (35). One wonders how a 4-year-old was able to know this by observing wings while Piper was not.
13. The wording that Todd Burpo uses here is somewhat puzzling. In other places, he takes great pains to show that he was constantly testing Colton's experience, asking questions he could not possibly know the answer to without a

first-hand experience of Heaven. Yet here he says that his testing of Colton was rare. Or did he mean that Colton answering correctly was rare. I'm not sure. I point it out merely in case the reader happened to have noticed the inconsistency.

14. The Bible does indeed teach that for the believer, to be absent from this body is to be present instantly with Jesus (Philippians 1:21; 2 Corinthians 5:8). What is interesting about this detail is that it is a direct contradiction to Don Piper's account. If we take Piper's account as true, then it is possible to be in Heaven for ninety minutes and never see Jesus. From Piper's account we learn that the first people we meet in Heaven will be our departed friends and family who were instrumental in bringing us to faith or in our discipleship. According to Piper, we actually meet them outside of Heaven's gate. They are our welcoming committee sent to usher us into God's presence. Didn't Piper realize that by endorsing this book, he was endorsing an account that serves to undermine his own credibility? Apparently not.

15. In the interests of space, I edited out some of the commentary and Todd's attempts to scramble together some Bible passages to support Colton's claim. I have kept in tact the essence of the conversation.

16. I would recommend John MacArthur's book *Safe In The Arms Of God*.

17. Emphasis mine.

18. The Akiane Gallary is located in Post Falls, Idaho. Her website http://www.artakiane.com/ gives samples of her paintings and contains the work of art that Colton would identify as a true representation of the Jesus he saw.

19. He also cites the apostle John as one who visited Heaven without dying.

20. This is given in detail in the book on page 78-79.

21. The translation given in *Heaven Is for Real* renders it as, "He heard inexpressible things, things that man is not permitted to tell."

Selling the Stairway to Heaven

86

3

A Critical Theological Review of
Proof of Heaven by Eben Alexander

If sales figures are any indication, Christians have been eager to purchase and promote the reports of those who claim to have been to Heaven and returned to tell us about it. *90 Minutes in Heaven* and *Heaven Is for Real* have proven to be wildly popular in Christian circles. This gullible lack of discernment presents us with an interesting dilemma: what do we do when someone who is clearly not a believer claims to have visited our Heaven and has returned to tell us about it?

Such is the case with *Proof of Heaven: A Neurosurgeon's Journey into the Afterlife* by Eben Alexander, M.D.[1]

Why This Review?

Why go through the pain of reading and reviewing yet another book about a trip to Heaven, especially since it was written by someone who makes no profession of orthodox faith in Christ and presents an experience of Heaven that is patently unbiblical?

First, I believe that this account, as unbiblical and counter-Christian as it is, has something to teach us concerning the credibility of those accounts more widely embraced by the Christian community. Understanding and explaining what Eben Alexander experienced from a Christian perspective can teach us some things about other supposed trips to Heaven and those who claim to have gone.

Second, accounts like that of Dr. Alexander point out a glaring inconsistency among Christians who embrace the stories of those more likely to spin a tale of their liking. This highlights the danger of embracing any such report of a visit to the afterlife. Alexander's journey shows that once the Pandora's Box of afterlife visitations is opened, one is hard-pressed to reject any spurious truth-claim and be consistent at the same time.

Third, skeptics of the Christian faith are quick to point out that many non-believers have near-death experiences which are in many ways similar to those described by Christians. What are we to make of this? Is there an explanation for it? If the Christian faith is true, then why and how do non-Christians have near-death experiences (NDEs) which include feelings of peace, tranquility, happiness, joy, and reunion with family members?

Alexander's journey into the afterlife is just such an account. What, from an orthodox Christian perspective, can explain a non-believer experiencing "Heaven"?

This review will be a bit different from my previous reviews of Don Piper and Todd Burpo's books. Those books were written by professing Christians and have enjoyed widespread acceptance within the Christian community. While *Proof of Heaven* is a New York Times bestseller, the book does not seem to have caught on within Christian circles to the extent that the Piper or Burpo books have. It seems this is largely due to the fact that the book does not even attempt to present a Christian view of God, the Bible, the soul, or the afterlife. It is a boldly non-Christian account of time in the afterlife. Therefore, this review will not be as thorough and meticulous as the previous reviews. I wish to deal with some broader issues and I am not as interested in contrasting Dr. Alexander's experience or teaching with

88

Scripture. That is unnecessary since he does not even claim to be representing biblical theology or to be promoting the Christian message.

His Spiritual Credentials

As far as I could tell from reading the book, Dr. Alexander has had no genuine conversion experience. By his own admission he attended "on occasion" his Episcopal church. He admits that:

> . . . for years I'd only been a step above a "C & E"er (one who only darkens the door of a church at Christmas and Easter). I encouraged our boys to say their prayers at night, but I was no spiritual leader in our home. I'd never escaped my feelings of doubt at how any of it could really be. As much as I'd grown up wanting to believe in God and Heaven and an afterlife, my decades in the rigorous scientific world of academic neurosurgery had profoundly called into question how such things could exist.[2]

Before his visit to the afterlife, Dr. Alexander was certainly no believer in God or Heaven.

> As a neurosurgeon, I'd heard many stories over the years of people who had strange experiences, usually after suffering cardiac arrest: stories of traveling to mysterious, wonderful landscapes; of talking to dead relatives— even of meeting God Himself. Wonderful stuff, no question. But all of it, in my opinion, was pure fantasy. What caused the otherworldly types of experiences that such people so often report? I didn't claim to know, but I did know that they were brain-based. All of consciousness is. If you don't have a working

89

brain, you can't be conscious (8).

On December 18, 2012, Dr. Alexander was interviewed on The Dennis Prager radio program. Prager asked, "Were you religiously active prior to the experience?"

Dr. Alexander answered by sharing what he records in the book about his atheism and then added, "So for 8 years before my experience I did not believe at all in a personal loving God or in any kind of benefit of prayer."[3]

In the same interview, he confesses his own belief in reincarnation saying that such belief makes sense in light of what he learned. He says that "reincarnation is important" in our quest to become divine.[4] He denies that the concept of eternal Hell makes any sense from the perspective of eternal and infinite love. Reincarnation is the way in which, he believes, justice is served.[5]

Alexander even says that Jesus Himself taught and believed in the doctrine of reincarnation. Prager asked, "So you have taken essentially the Buddhist view that, (pause) and the Hindu view of karma?"

Alexander responded:

Well, I would, . . . I think that is certainly part of it. I would also say that I think, . . . uh . . ., certainly being, . . . having grown up a Christian that I'm . . . uh, quite convinced now especially having read the gnostic gospels and become much more familiar with the teaching, the Christian teachings in their pure form, you know not necessarily filtered through the counsels of centuries later, that in fact, Jesus knew very well of reincarnation, of course, He is a prime example of reincarnation.[6]

That statement is so full of error, bad theology, and other problems that I could write a chapter on it alone!

As a result of his experience, Dr. Alexander did come to believe that our human consciousness does continue beyond the grave. He writes:

My experience showed me that the death of the body and the brain are not the end of consciousness, that human experience continues beyond the grave. More important, it continues under the gaze of a God who loves and cares about each one of us and about where the universe itself and all the beings within it are ultimately going (9).

Such a transformation from atheism to theism does not a Christian make. He called himself a Christian on the Dennis Prager program, but what he actually believes is anything but Christian theology and orthodoxy.

As a former skeptic, he feels uniquely qualified to tell his story to those "who might have heard stories similar to mine before and wanted to believe them, but had not been able to full do so." He wants to tell his story to "these people, more than any other" (10).

As you will see below, his NDE did not bring him to a knowledge of the one true and living God revealed in Scripture.

An Overview: The Story in a Nutshell

Eben Alexander earned his M.D. from Duke University Medical School in 1980 where he also did his residency. For 15 years he worked at Harvard Medical School and Brigham & Women's Hospital in Boston. In 2008 while living in Lynchburg, Virginia he was a neurosurgeon at the Focused Ultrasound Surgery Foundation in Charlottesville.

On November 10, 2008, Eben suddenly awoke at 4:30 a.m. with back pain that had been bothering him the previous evening. He thought it was the results of a flu virus that was still hanging on. He tried getting out of bed and easing the pain with a warm bath, but it only intensified. By 6:30 that morning he was lying in agony and virtually paralyzed. He soon slipped into unconsciousness. Thinking he was napping, his wife left him so he could rest. After two hours, she returned to find his body stiff and jerking violently.

EMTs rushed him to Lynchburg General Hospital Emergency Room. Diagnosing his own episode he writes, "Had I been conscious, I could have told Holley [his wife] exactly what I was undergoing there on the bed during those terrifying moments she spent waiting for the ambulance: a full grand mal seizure, brought on, no doubt, by some kind of extremely severe shock to my brain" (16).

As doctors would soon discover, Dr. Alexander had bacterial meningitis. His brain and spinal column were infected with Escherichia Coli, commonly called E-Coli.

For the next seven days Eben Alexander remained unconscious to the world around him. During that week, Eben claims he visited Heaven and came to understand the profound mysteries of the unseen world and the universe in which we live.

Now he is back to tell you all about it.

The Afterlife of Eben

Eben's description of his trip to "Heaven" is in no way similar to that given by either Colton Burpo or Don Piper.

His first awareness in the afterlife was of a surrounding darkness. He was not aware of having a body. He felt as if he were surrounded by dirty gelatin. The darkness was almost suffocating. He heard a deep rhythmic pounding which sounded distant. He calls this place "Realm of the Earthworm's-Eye View."

He originally felt like he was one with this subterranean world. But gradually this sense gave way to a different feeling. He slowly realized he was trapped in this world he was experiencing. He describes "grotesque animal faces" which "bubbled out of the muck, groaned or screeched, and then were gone again" (31).

The more he became aware of his surroundings, the more he began to panic and he realized that he needed to get out.

> The more I began to feel like a *me*- like something separate from the cold and wet and dark around me - the more the faces that bubbled up out of that darkness became ugly and threatening. The rhythmic pounding off in the distance sharpened and intensified as well - became the work-beat for some army of troll-like underground laborers, performing some endless, brutally monotonous task. The movement around me became less visual and more tactile, as if reptilian, wormlike creatures were crowding past, occasionally rubbing up against me with their smooth or spiky skins. Then I became aware of a smell: a little like feces, a little like blood, and a little like vomit (31).

He claims he was delivered from this realm of darkness by a "white-gold light" (38). With a whooshing sound he found himself in a completely new world. He saw a countryside and a realm that was very earthlike, complete with dogs, trees, fields, streams, waterfalls, children and people who sang and danced in circles.

Suddenly he realized he was not alone but was accompanied by a beautiful girl.[7] They were riding together on an intricately patterned surface which he realized was the wing of a butterfly. There were millions of butterflies all around them.

The girl finally spoke to him, though without words. "The message went through me like a wind, and I instantly understood that it was true (40).

What did this divine messenger say?

The message had three parts, and if I had to translate them into earthly language, I'd say they ran something like this:

"You are loved and cherished, dearly, forever.

"You have nothing to fear.

"There is nothing you can do wrong."

The message flooded me with a vast and crazy sensation of relief. It was like being handed the rules to a game I'd been playing all my life without ever fully understanding it (41).

These three messages are repeated throughout the course of the book (71). These three things are central in Dr. Alexander's understanding of the meaning of life and what God would have us to know. Or as Alexander notes, "The unconditional love and acceptance that I experienced on my journey is the single most important discovery I have ever made, or will ever make, . . ." (73). Later he writes, "The very fabric of the alternate dimension is love and acceptance, and anything that does not have these qualities appears immediately and obviously out of place there" (73).

This is the "gospel" (the good news) of Dr. Alexander's experience of the afterlife.

What of God?

No visit to the afterlife would be complete without some experience of the divine. Alexander's visit is no exception. At one point in his journey, he claims to have entered an immense void, which was pitch black and yet brimming over with light. (I know, I'm shaking my head too.)

The light was coming from a brilliant orb that he sensed nearby. He claims:

My situation was, strangely enough, something akin to that of a fetus in a womb. The fetus floats in the womb with the silent partner of the placenta, which nourishes it and mediates its relationship to the everywhere present yet at the same time invisible mother. In this case, the "mother" was God, the Creator, the Source who is responsible for making the universe and all in it. This Being was so close that there seemed to be no distance at all between God and myself. Yet at the same time, I could sense the infinite vastness of the Creator, could see how completely minuscule I was by comparison. I will occasionally use Om as the pronoun for God because I originally used that name in my writings after my coma. "Om" was the sound I remembered hearing associated with that omniscient, omnipotent, and unconditionally loving God, but any descriptive word falls short (47).

The "orb" was not God. Alexander claims that though the "Being" of God was close he still required the orb to act as an "interpreter." Through this interpreter, Alexander claims that he was given certain revelations regarding the universe and other dimensions. "While beyond my body, I received knowledge about the nature and structure of the universe that was vastly beyond my comprehension" (81).

Whenever one rejects God as He has revealed Himself in Scripture, they will inevitably replace Him with a god of their own creation.[8] That god will always be a lot like its creator. The god of Dr. Alexander's experience is shockingly like Dr. Alexander himself. For instance, he says:

One of the biggest mistakes people make when they think about God is to imagine God as impersonal. Yes, God is behind the numbers, the perfection of the universe that science measures and struggles to understand. But - again, paradoxically - Om is "human" as well - even more human than you and I are. Om understands and sympathizes with our human situation more profoundly and personally than we can even imagine because Om knows what we have forgotten, and understands the terrible burden it is to live with amnesia of the Divine for even a moment (85-86).

I'm not exactly sure what he means by that, but I am sure that it is utter nonsense!

A Theology of Evil

Alexander's understanding of the reality and purpose of moral evil in our world betrays a very New Age and Eastern view of reality.

Through the Orb, Om told me that there is not one universe but many— in fact, more than I could conceive— but that love lay at the center of them all. Evil was present in all the other universes as well, but only in the tiniest trace amounts. Evil was necessary because without it free will was

96

impossible, and without free will there could be no growth— no forward movement, no chance for us to become what God longed for us to be. Horrible and all-powerful as evil sometimes seemed to be in a world like ours, in the larger picture love was overwhelmingly dominant, and it would ultimately be triumphant. I saw the abundance of life throughout the countless universes, including some whose intelligence was advanced far beyond that of humanity. I saw that there are countless higher dimensions, but that the only way to know these dimensions is to enter and experience them directly. They cannot be known, or understood, from lower dimensional space. Cause and effect exist in these higher realms, but outside of our earthly conception of them. The world of time and space in which we move in this terrestrial realm is tightly and intricately meshed within these higher worlds. In other words, these worlds aren't totally apart from us, because all worlds are part of the same overarching divine Reality. From those higher worlds one could access any time or place in our world (48-49).

As you can see, Alexander says that evil is a necessity in our universe because without evil, there could be no "free will."[9] "That evil could occasionally have the upper hand was known and allowed by the Creator as a necessary consequence of giving the gift of free will to beings like us" (83).[10]

Apparently this life of making moral choices allows us to gradually acquire salvation and earn rank in the dimension to come. "Free will is of central importance for our function in the earthly realm: a function that, we will all one day discover, serves the much higher role of allowing our ascendance in the timeless alternate dimension" (84). By making good moral choices in the presence of so much evil, we "grow toward the Divine" (84).[11]

This is the closest thing to a doctrine of salvation that Alexander presents: we are evolutionary beings, evolved from the earth, who face moral decisions and live through evil, and manifest love and compassion to earn ascendancy in another dimension. He promises, "In order to return to that realm, we must once again become like that realm, even while we are stuck in, and plodding through, this one" (85).

There is a clear inconsistency between Dr. Alexander's understanding of moral evil and human sinfulness. You may remember that the "guardian angel" (102) on the butterfly wing told him that he could do no wrong. He later recalled this to mind:

. . . When I was in the Core, there was never any worry or guilt about letting anyone down. That had, of course, been one of the first things that I'd learned when I was with the Girl on the Butterfly Wing and she'd told me: "There is nothing you can do that is wrong" (109).

He seems to think that this is true of all people, since he holds this out as a great lesson - a truth - to be learned from his time in the afterlife. But if there is nothing that he can do that is wrong, and therefore guilt is an illegitimate fabrication of human conscience, then what is evil? If nobody can do anything wrong, then nobody can do evil. If evil is not possible for anyone to do, then in what sense are they "free" by his own definition of "freedom?" How does one wrestle through making "right" choices to gain ascendancy in other dimensions if there is no possibility of one making a "wrong" choice? Ultimately, EVERY unbiblical worldview will die the death of self contradiction. This one certainly does.

To be fair, Dr. Alexander seems to be aware of the moral inconsistency in his own presentation. In the interview with Dennis Prager he recalled the three things that the angelic messenger had told him, but the third one he stated as, "There is nothing you can do wrong in this realm."[12]

Prager immediately sensed a moral problem and quickly jumped in with, "What does that mean? You can do nothing wrong in which realm?"

Alexander said:

Well, . . . what. . . what it meant at the time was that you could do nothing wrong in that spiritual realm.. . . because. . . the issue though is in fact, though, uh. . . strictly speaking her words apply to earth too if you realize that we are here to manifest that unconditional and infinite love of the creator for fellow beings in spite of the injustice and imperfections of this realm and realize we can either do that in our free will and choices and follow very directly towards that deification in the outer realm or we can not do that and we can dish out evil and pain and mayhem."[13]

It is still unclear to me what he means. The book gives no such qualification or explanation, nor does it limit the angel's words to "that realm." Even his explanation on the radio program admits that this applies to earth. Though he tried to avoid this moral contradiction, in the end he is back where he started.

This betrays his Eastern and New Age theology. He believes that evil is not something done by humans for which we are accountable. Evil is something outside of us, some force, some power. According to his theology, evil is not something we are, it is something outside us that afflicts us.

And So Much More!

What you have just read is only a sampling - and a very selective one at that - of the horrible theology and unbiblical worldview promoted by *Proof of Heaven*. We could analyze his statements about meditation, prayer, universalism, and the soul, but what we have examined is sufficient to show that Dr. Alexander is certainly no Christian believer. His theology is not Christian theology, his world-view is not a Christian worldview and his experience of "Heaven" is nothing like that described in Scripture.

The book mentions Jesus only three times; once in the title of a book contained in the bibliography, once as the subject of a painting in his church, and once in a description of someone else's NDE.

Clearly this is a decidedly non-Christian account of an NDE and journey to the afterlife.

What They All Have in Common

Dr. Eben Alexander claims to have had an experience out of his body in another dimension which is indicative of the actual afterlife that all of us will one day experience.

Like Burpo and Piper[14], Dr. Alexander seems convinced that his experience is real. However, the experience that he is convinced he had and the "Heaven" he describes is nothing like that of Burpo or Piper.

These three experiences do have a number of things in common.

First, they are all untestable. These experiences are experiences. We can't measure the light they describe, or validate the experiences by some scientific method.

Second, they cannot be verified. All of these experiences were singular experiences of one person. Nobody went to Heaven with Piper. Nobody accompanied Alexander. There are no witnesses for these experiences. We are expected to take these men at their word and nothing more.

Third, all of these supposed accounts contradict Scripture at a number of points.[15] This only serves to undermine the authority of Scripture, its credibility, and the reader's belief in its sufficiency. Not only do they all contradict Scripture, but they all contradict one another. We are forced to choose between believing either Piper or Burpo or Alexander or the Bible. They cannot all be giving us the truth!

Fourth, all three of them appear equally convinced that their experience was real and that it presents an accurate picture of Heaven. Dr. Alexander offers a very picturesque, vivid and colorful description of what he saw and experienced. It seems that it is as "real" as anything he has experienced in this earth in his body. There can be no doubt that those who promote these experiences appear convinced that they are real experiences that accurately reflect reality.[16]

Christians would be far less likely to embrace the testimony of Dr. Alexander than they would of either Piper or Burpo. If Dr. Alexander's experience is a true and accurate account of reality, then the Bible is clearly wrong. The Christian doctrines of sin, salvation, Heaven, Hell, eternal punishment, the soul of man, evil, Jesus, and Trinitarianism cannot be true if Dr. Alexander's experience is.

Thinking through Some Possibilities

I am forced to conclude that the testimony of Dr. Alexander must be rejected. But on what grounds? I cannot reject his account simply because he is not "one of us" (meaning "evangelical Christian"). I have to reject it because it disagrees with Scripture.[17] If Scripture is my standard then Scripture ALONE gives me the truth concerning spiritual realities, including the afterlife. Experience is no sure measure of spiritual truth.

The question still remains, "How do we explain the experience of Dr. Alexander from a Biblical perspective?"[18] There are a few different possible explanations.

Explanation #1: Dr. Alexander is lying.

It is entirely possible that Eben Alexander has fabricated the entire experience.[19] It is possible that he doesn't actually believe that any of this happened and knows full well that every word he wrote concerning his "experience" is a well-crafted lie.

For the record, I do believe that Alexander had some sort of experience and that he is absolutely convinced that he had that experience. I don't believe he has fabricated this entire account. Though I do not believe that he is lying, we must admit this as a possibility.

Unlike either Burpo or Piper, Dr. Alexander entirely lacked a financial motivation for fabricating the account. Alexander is a very intelligent neurosurgeon with a well-paying job in a nice part of the country. There is nothing from his story that makes me think that there existed any substantial drive to profit from his story, though I do not doubt that he has.

It is also worth noting that to promote this lie, Alexander would be forced to abandon his formerly materialistic worldview and admit that he had been wrong.

He is a medical doctor who did not believe that God existed or that there is an afterlife. He denied the supernatural and the immortality of the soul. He believed and taught that everything could be explained in terms of chemical reactions within the brain and neurological processes. He did not believe that soul and body were separate and distinct from one another.

Dr. Alexander has publicly abandoned and repudiated that former worldview.[20] I would suggest that only an experience that he genuinely believes to be true could cause him to do this and suffer whatever consequences might come his way.

Further, he lived and worked among peers who, generally speaking, shared that same worldview. Speaking out about this experience would make him something of a pariah among his colleagues. He could not expect that sharing his story would make him a celebrity among those in his field.[21]

Explanation #2: It was a vivid hallucination.

It seems that given the toxicity of the infection of his brain and spine, and given the medications with which he was treated, the possibility that this was all a very elaborate and vivid hallucination should at least be on the table.

Alexander entertains this as a possibility in *Appendix B: Neuroscientific Hypotheses I Considered to Explain My Experiences*. In the fourth of the nine suggested explanations, Dr. Alexander says that the area of his brain required to produces hallucinations was shut down and badly damaged by the bacterial meningitis (174).

This may be true and it might be enough to rule out a vivid hallucination, but Dr. Alexander's rejection of that hypothesis assumes that the brain is necessary for hallucinations. It assumes that our soul/mind cannot experience anything apart from the accompanying chemical reactions within the brain. His book admits the opposite, that there is a higher or different reality that is not connected to our brain which he claims to have visited and experienced.

So while he may be right to say that there is no physical, neurological cause for an hallucination, he cannot dismiss a spiritual explanation for an hallucination. We can only know for sure that a chemical reaction did not cause it in the particular area of the brain (the neocortex), that we currently believe to be responsible for hallucinations. However, we must admit that it might still be an hallucination caused by something else which we may not know anything about at this time.

We should not assume that every hallucination requires a chemical reaction within the physical brain or even the brain itself. We are conscious, immaterial beings who exist independent of our physical brains.

If man is only a material being then of course there is no spirit/mind part of man that can experience anything without an accompanying physical or chemical process. But man is not merely a material being. We have an eternal soul/mind which can certainly experience things not connected to our physical body. Dr. Alexander admits this in arguing that he saw and experienced the afterlife outside of and apart from His body. Dr. Alexander admits there is a reality that is not merely physical which we can experience apart from our body. Then he dismisses the possibility of an hallucination by saying that it cannot happen apart from the body. This is a clear contradiction in his own view.

Explanation #3: Dr. Alexander's experience was a demonic deception.

This is what I believe happened.

104

Alexander admits that we are spiritual beings. He talks in the book about the mistake of assuming that there is no greater spiritual reality. The Heaven he claims to visit is one populated with spirit beings, one of which he calls his "guardian angel." Given just the experiences that he has had, he would have to admit that it is a possibility that these spiritual beings were evil and that they have grandly deceived him concerning the afterlife.

From a Christian perspective this is not at all difficult to admit. The Bible teaches that there are a host of demonic beings, fallen angels who war against God, His people, and His truth. These demonic beings are intent on deceiving people and blinding them to the truth. Their chief is a fallen angel named Satan who "disguises himself as an angel of light" (2 Cor. 11:14). He is the father of lies and a liar from the beginning (John 8:44).

Satan delights in deceiving people concerning the truth about sin, salvation, God, Heaven, and Hell.

It is not at all difficult to believe that Satan could create an experience in the conscious mind of an unbeliever (who is his child) and use the infection, the drugs, his memories, and demons to do so. Such an experience could be vivid, memorable, and very real.

"To what end?" we might ask. To promote lies concerning God, evil, sin, salvation, and Heaven. The Devil blasphemes God, Heaven, and the people of God (Revelation 13:6). Dr. Alexander's account, however real it seems to him, is but lies concerning the eternal realities of Heaven, Hell, God, and salvation.

People who believe Dr. Alexander's account of Heaven must at the same time reject what Scripture says about it. He presents a New Age, unbiblical view of evil, sin, and moral responsibility. The god he describes is not the God of the

105

Bible. He offers a salvation apart from Jesus Christ and an afterlife absent any divine justice. This can only serve to undermine the credibility of Scripture and any belief in its infallibility or sufficiency.

Alexander's experience is a tool used by the prince of darkness to deceive people about the true Heaven. What he teaches about God is a lie. What he teaches about sin is a lie. What he teaches about the afterlife is a lie. Therefore, by implication, what he teaches about Scripture is a lie. If Alexander is to be believed, the Bible is not.

The father of lies is the devil himself. The result of this deception has been the peddling and telling of lies to millions about life's ultimate realities. Satan has a vested interest in that.

I believe that this third explanation fits all the details of this account. It explains how this experience could be perceived as so real, vivid, and memorable. It explains why Dr. Alexander would reverse his worldview and come to an understanding of reality completely contrary to his former thinking. It explains how he could have an experience so filled with error, but one he is so convinced is truth. It is consistent with a biblical worldview.

A Christian Inconsistency

Stories like the one told by Dr. Alexander expose the inconsistent thinking of the undiscerning Christian community. The Christian who believes the testimony of Don Piper or Colton Burpo has no grounds for rejecting the testimony of Eben Alexander.

If you believe that God allows people to visit the afterlife and then return to tell the rest of us about it, how can you say that Eben Alexander did not experience such a visit?

106

"Well," one may argue, "Dr. Alexander's story is so clearly unbiblical and filled with lies." How do you know the same is not true of Burpo and Piper? They relate things which we are not told in Scripture and other things which clearly contradict it. If fidelity to Scripture is the standard, then all three accounts must be rejected.

If we are willing to entertain the possibility that Dr. Alexander is lying, then why shouldn't we consider that the same might be true of both Don Piper and Colton/Todd Burpo? If it is likely that Alexander was deceived by the devil through his experience, why shouldn't we consider that the same might be true of the others?

A More Excellent Way

Is there a better way for Christians to view these supposed trips to Heaven that is consistent and true to Scripture? Yes.

First, we affirm that there is a Heaven and a Hell because that is what Scripture teaches.

Second, we believe this based upon the testimony of Scripture and not the experiences of people who claim to have had visions, dreams or trips to Heaven. We believe in these realities because Jesus Christ spoke of them, not because Don Piper visited there.

Third, we can reject the spurious, anecdotal, and unbiblical testimonies of all these men with complete consistency. The fact that they tell a story which seems to match the teaching of Scripture more closely is no reason to believe what they say while rejecting others.

I don't need Don Piper, Colton Burpo, or Eben Alexander to tell me that Heaven is real. I know it is real because Jesus Christ has told me so in Scripture. I don't doubt His word one bit. Their testimony is completely

107

unnecessary. Don Piper can add nothing to the truthfulness of Jesus Christ. Colton Burpo sheds no light or understanding on the truth of God's Word. The Word of God and the testimony of Jesus Christ do not need to be authenticated by these men's fanciful tales. They lend no credibility to the Lord of Glory and Truth - Jesus Christ.

Summary

Eben Alexander presents an account of the afterlife completely at odds with the biblical teaching of God, sin, salvation, and Heaven. It is an account filled with lies about these eternal realities. The most viable explanation for Dr. Alexander's experience is that he is genuinely convinced what he saw is true because he has been successfully deceived by the father of lies.

Dr. Alexander's account, which would be rightly rejected by Bible-believing Christians presents an interesting dilemma for those same Christians who would accept the testimony of Don Piper or Colton Burpo. Consistency and biblical fidelity require that we reject the testimony of all three men. Such accounts are neither true to the biblical text nor are they necessary for faith. They only serve to undermine belief in Scripture as the sole rule for life and godliness.

Endnotes

1. You can see some videos and read about the author at his website: http://www.lifebeyonddeath.net/.

2. Alexander III M.D., Eben (2012-10-23). *Proof of Heaven: A Neurosurgeon's Journey into the Afterlife* (p. 34). Simon & Schuster. Kindle Edition. From this point forward I will include page numbers from this book in parentheses.

3. You can see Prager's page on the interview at http://www.dennisprager.com/alexander-proof-of-heaven/. For a full audio recording of that interview you can visit the American Conservative University Podcast and listen at http://acu.libsyn.com/show-proof-of-heaven-a-neurosurgeon-s-journey-into-the-afterlife (approx. 14:00 mark).

4. Time mark 22:45-23:10.

5. Time mark 33:45-34:00.

6. Time mark 30:00-32:00.

7. On page 102 he refers to this beautiful girl as his "guardian angel."

8. This is a violation of the first and second commandments.

9. Obviously he believes that men who do evil are "free." However, the Bible teaches that all men are slaves of sin who love darkness and are at war with God. He never attempts to answer the obvious dilemma that his view presents, namely, if there is no evil in the life to come, will we be truly free? If evil does not exist in Heaven, then does God rob us of our freedom to preserve a perfect Heaven? If God cherished human freedom so much in this life that He would allow evil, why would He not care about human freedom in the life to come? For more on this, see "Answering the Problem of Evil" available at http://kootenaichurch.org/newsletters/ miscellaneous/.

10. Biblically speaking, evil never has "the upper hand." It is always under the sovereign control of a God who uses it to accomplish the good of His people and the glory of His name.

11. In this same location, Alexander asserts that we currently inhabit "evolutionarily developed mortal brains and bodies, the product of the earth and the exigencies of the earth."

12. Emphasis added. See the link for the interview in footnote 3. This statement is at the 17:30 mark and following.

13. Time mark 18:00-19:00.

14. Don Piper wrote *90 Minutes in Heaven* and Todd Burpo wrote *Heaven Is for Real*. Interestingly, Alexander lists Piper's book, *90 Minutes in Heaven* on his reading list at the end of his book. I have no doubt that he would have included *Heaven Is for Real* on that list if it had been published at the time Alexander published his book. Alexander seems not the least bit disturbed by the fact that the "Heaven" described by Piper is radically different than that which he experienced.

15. For specific details I would point you to the respective reviews.

16. Burpo titled his book *Heaven Is for Real* and Don Piper describes his experience as "the most real thing that has ever happened to me."

17. The same standard forces me to reject the accounts of Burpo and Piper as well. Their contradictions to Scripture are numerous and documented. Yet Christians embrace the stories of Piper and Burpo while rejecting those similar to Alexander. I ask, "On what grounds?" Piper and Burpo are just as egotistical in their story-telling, dismissive of and careless with Scripture, and contradictory to the Bible as Alexander.

18. The following would apply not just to Dr. Alexander's account, but also all others who have had NDEs.

19. I am not speaking here of his bacterial meningitis or 7-day coma, but only his NDE.

20. This is not the case with Piper or Burpo. Claiming that they made a trip to Heaven did not require that they abandon anything that they had previously believed. Both of them already believed in Heaven, in God, and in the immortality of the soul. In fact, their descriptions of "Heaven" are amazingly similar to that

which they had already believed about Heaven. They learned nothing new during their trips which required a radical rewrite of their previously-held beliefs. (In the case of Burpo, Todd, who wrote the book, learned nothing about Heaven from Colton, who visited Heaven, that he did not already believe.)

21. Just the opposite is the case with Piper and Burpo. Their "trips to Heaven" have been very lucrative endeavors, catapulting both of them to celebrity status in the Christian community. They have appeared on countless radio and TV programs, their calendars have been booked with speaking engagements and interviews and they have been greeted with anything but skepticism and rejection by the Christian community.

4

Conclusion:
The Problems with Heaven Tourism

"Heaven Tourism" is all the rage. It used to be that we had to rely upon charismatic leaders to regale us with fanciful tales of visits to Heaven and one-on-one conversations with God. Now such phenomena have become fully mainstream within non-charismatic circles, due in large part to the accounts of Baptist pastor Don Piper and Methodist pastor Todd Burpo. Kevin Malarkey contributes his recently recanted account of a trip to Heaven in *The Boy Who Came Back from Heaven*. Even a self-confessed rank pagan, Eben Alexander, claims to have made the trip in *Proof of Heaven*. In fact, a search on Amazon for "heaven visit" will pull up a nauseatingly long list of books offering first-hand accounts of trips to Heaven. It is a profitable business indeed!

In the three previous chapters, I have offered lengthy, detailed theological critiques of three bestsellers from this genre. In this chapter, I will address the problems with these claims in a more general way. Each of those books presents its own unique set of issues and shortcomings; however, there are problems raised by all of these reports. There are serious issues that all of them have in common.

We can summarize these shared problems under four headings. First, they do not fit the biblical pattern. Second, they do not reflect biblical priorities. Third, they contradict clear biblical teaching. Fourth, they do not honor biblical revelation.

They Do Not Fit the Biblical Pattern

Visions, Not Visitations

In all of redemptive history and inspired Scripture, there were only four men who were allowed to see into Heaven: Isaiah (Isaiah 6), Stephen (Acts 7:54-60), Paul (2 Corinthians 12:1-10), and John (Revelation 4-21).

In none of those instances did the person die, go to Heaven, and then return to tell about it. Each of these was a vision of Heaven, not a visit to Heaven. Not even Stephen was an exception. He had his vision while dying, but he did not die and then come back to report on his experience. None of the four men who had visions of Heaven did so while their bodies were unconscious, ill, or dead.

Contrast that with Don Piper's claim that he was dead for a full ninety minutes while he was in Heaven, at the end of which time he was resurrected. In the cases of both Burpo and Alexander, they claim they visited Heaven while their bodies were being medically treated.

Clearly, the experiences and claims of modern visitors to Heaven are of a completely different nature than those described in Scripture. The biblical pattern is of visions, not visitations.

Silence from Sources

The Bible does give accounts of men and women who were seriously ill and then healed, as well as a few who were resurrected, yet interestingly, none of them offer an account of the afterlife! None of those who were seriously ill and healed reported that, while ill, they visited Heaven. Of those few people in Scripture who were resurrected, none of them offers details of his time in the afterlife. Scripture does not record any of them relating the sights and sounds of Heaven.

112

The fact that Scripture gives no testimony concerning the nature and features of Heaven or Hell from the lips of those who died and returned to life suggests that such testimony was deemed either unreliable or unimportant. It is also possible that those who came back from the dead were kept from remembering any of the details of their time in Heaven.

Lazarus was raised from the dead after four days in Heaven, but we have no record of his time there. Did the Spirit of God overlook something in His writing of the account that was necessary for us? Are we to trust Don Piper to fill in where the Holy Spirit lacks? Perhaps this silence is due to the fact that Lazarus had no memory of his time in Heaven while dead. Perhaps God did not want us to hear testimony from such a source. Whatever the reason, we can certainly see that modern claims of trips to Heaven do not fit the biblical pattern.

Dearth of Details

Of the four men in Scripture who did have visions of Heaven, three of them are VERY scant on the details. The Apostle John's revelation of Heaven is by far the most detailed and was specifically given for that purpose.

Isaiah's vision of Heaven is contained in one short chapter out of 66 that focuses mostly on the glory of God, Isaiah's response to that glory, and his subsequent commission. Stephen's vision of Heaven receives a brief mention with only a few details. Of the 13 books in the New Testament authored by Paul, his account is only mentioned briefly in one of them: 2 Corinthians. Even there, Paul offers the experience as a defense of his apostolic credentials, and only reluctantly. His hand was forced. Paul offers no description of sights and sounds other than to say that he "heard inexpressible words, which a man is not permitted to speak" (12:4). He offered no details, since Paul did not regard such visions as the least bit profitable for the Church. Surely if Paul thought such visions of Heaven were of any profit to anyone, he would have related the details on more than one occasion to more than one audience. He did not. Yet Piper and Burpo continue to tell their tales on any occasion to any audience, and have profited quite handsomely from it. The Burpos have even turned their tale into a major motion picture. I cannot imagine the Apostle Paul doing the same. In fact, he did the exact opposite.

Whereas the great Apostle Paul did not regard such visions as worth more than a mere mention, Piper views himself as God's messenger to the Church to confirm Scripture and offer assurance to those who doubt it. Paul did not regard it as profitable. Piper suggests such visions are essential. Paul was silent about his experience and Piper sings like a canary on steroids. The two approaches could not be more opposite.

The modern-day accounts of Heaven Tourism do not fit the biblical pattern.

They Do Not Reflect Biblical Priorities

No gospel

One feature that relentlessly plagues these accounts of alleged trips to Heaven is the complete lack of a gospel presentation. Neither Don Piper nor Todd Burpo give anything close to what might be considered a gospel presentation in their books.

Piper claims that after his alleged trip to Heaven he feels a stronger sense of responsibility to make the way absolutely clear (129). Yet in 205 pages of his account, there is nothing that even approaches a clear gospel presentation.

Burpo fails even more miserably, making a complete hash out of the theology of the cross.

If God were going to give modern-day revelations of the realities of Heaven to someone, don't you think He would do it to someone able to present the biblical gospel? Don't you think He would choose people who understood the gospel and could clearly communicate it? Either these men do not know what the gospel is (having never embraced it themselves), they are ashamed of it (fearing that a clear gospel presentation would offend readers and hinder sales) or this is a tragic oversight bordering on dereliction of duty. Since both men have had ample opportunity after the initial publishing of their works to correct any oversight, we have to assume it is one of the first two options.

No glory

When Isaiah saw a vision of Heaven, he recounted the staggering glory that was on display. The train of God's robe filled the temple. The foundations and thresholds trembled. Angels were saying, "Holy, Holy, Holy is the Lord of hosts, the whole earth is full of His glory." When Isaiah saw Heaven and saw the Lord of Hosts, he was undone. He cried out, "Woe is me, for I am ruined! Because I am a man of unclean lips, and I live among a people of unclean lips" (Isaiah 6:5). He was overwhelmed with his own sinfulness. He could not stand.

When Colton Burpo went to Heaven, he sat on Jesus' lap and Jesus helped him with his homework. Colton marveled over Jesus' rainbow-colored horse and recounts that the Holy Spirit is blue. Burpo claims that Colton sat on a chair in God's throne room and saw Jesus standing at God's right hand and Gabriel sitting on God's left hand. He even claims that he sat by God, the Holy Spirit. Likewise, Piper offers no indication that he was overwhelmed with the

115

glory and holiness of God while in Heaven. To Piper it was all like a big family reunion.

The glory of God and His holiness are central features of the biblical description of Heaven. They are mysteriously absent from the accounts of modern Heaven tourists.

No God

Piper states in his book that he never saw Jesus or the Father. In fact, he admits that he never actually went into Heaven. His ninety minutes were spent just outside the gate, visiting with his welcoming committee.

Piper presents a Heaven without God. Yet Piper insists that his experience was one of peace, love, tranquility, joy, and delights beyond our imagination. All of this without one moment in the presence of God.

The biblical priorities of God, His glory, and His gospel are nowhere to be found in the accounts of those who claim to have visited Heaven. Those things which are central priorities of Heaven get scant mention in the tales of those who supposedly went there.

They Contradict Clear Biblical Teaching

All the accounts of Heaven Tourism that I have read contain details concerning Heaven that contradict things found in Scripture. More than that, the whole idea that men go to Heaven and return to tell about it contradicts clear statements in Scripture.

John 3:13: "No one has ascended into Heaven, but He who descended from Heaven: the Son of Man." That verse comes in the context of Jesus' conversation with Nicodemus. He had explained heavenly truth to Nicodemus and challenged Nicodemus to believe His testimony. Jesus had told him that entrance to the Kingdom of Heaven required a new birth since the Kingdom of Heaven is a spiritual reality.

"That which is born of the flesh is flesh" and thus unable to see the Kingdom. These are easily-understood earthly realities. But Nicodemus did not believe them. Jesus said, "If I told you earthly things and you do not believe, how will you believe if I tell you heavenly things?"

Jesus is uniquely qualified to speak of the realities of Heaven, since He came from Heaven and He was going back to Heaven. So He said, "No man has ascended to Heaven, but He who descended from Heaven."

No man has ascended to Heaven. Did Jesus mean "no man" or did He mean "no man except Colton Burpo, Don Piper, and a host of other people who are now qualified to come back and speak to us about heavenly things"? "No man has ascended to Heaven." Either Jesus was correct, ignorant, or worse yet, He was lying. If we are to believe the accounts of Heaven Tourism, then we must conclude that either Jesus was ignorant and did not know that it was possible for men to ascend to Heaven and come back, or He was lying to Nicodemus.

It might be argued that that was true at the time, but since that statement, people have ascended to Heaven.

Why should we believe that things have changed? Why should we believe that we are now able to do something we were unable to do till the time of Christ? Remember that even after Jesus' words in John 3, no man ascended to Heaven. John, Paul, and Stephen all had visions of Heaven without visiting Heaven. None of them "ascended" to Heaven and came back. We have no record in Scripture of a man going to Heaven and coming back, and there is no reason to believe that anything has changed. Why should I believe that Heaven is now open to visitors, or that men are now able to do what they were unable to do before?

117

Further, Jesus was claiming in that statement that He alone is uniquely qualified to speak of heavenly realities since He had been in Heaven and now had descended from Heaven. Are we really to believe that Piper and Burpo are now in this elite class of qualified spokesmen? It is pretty egomaniacal for someone to suggest that they are as qualified as Jesus to reveal the secrets of Heaven.

Hebrews 9:27: "And inasmuch as it is appointed for men to die once and after this comes judgment." Unless your name is Burpo or Piper, then you die twice?

Someone might argue that there are obviously exceptions to this statement. Not only did Lazarus (John 11) die twice, but there were others who were resurrected in Scripture who ended up dying a second time as well.

That is true, but all of those accounts took place before Hebrews was written. The author seems to say, without hesitation and without exception, that men die only once. He certainly did not expect that exceptions such as Lazarus would continue to occur in the future. Why should I believe the reports of men who claim to be the exception to what God has appointed?

They Do Not Honor Biblical Revelation

I have already pointed out in the separate reviews that both Piper and Burpo have pathetically low views of Scripture. Piper's book suggests that unbelief regarding the testimony of Scripture is completely excusable and that we should be so thankful that he has been permitted to confirm Scripture for us. Even the very title of Burpo's book is an affront to thinking Christians: *Heaven Is for Real*. Did we really need the testimony of a 4-year-old boy to convince us of that? The reason these men wrote books to convince, encourage, and assure us of the reality of Heaven is because

118

they believe that Scripture is not sufficient to do so. Since Scripture is insufficient, they expect their testimonies to buttress our faith.

Just as problematic is the fact that such experiences of Heaven amount to nothing less than an authoritative revelation. How else could they be understood? If Colton Burpo saw Heaven, and what he and his father, Todd, wrote in the book is true, then it is just as authoritative and inspired as Romans or Revelation. How can it be otherwise? If he went to Heaven, it can only be because God allowed it and revealed it. Therefore Colton's account is divine revelation.

God cannot reveal truth less accurately on one occasion than He does on another. So if something in Piper or Burpo's books contradict Scripture, then whom do we have to blame? Did God get something wrong? Did Piper? Did the Apostle John? Do we edit the book of Revelation so as to make it conform to this newly revealed truth in *90 Minutes*?

Should we add these books to the end of our Bibles? Should we read chapters from them in our worship service as we read chapters from Romans or Isaiah? If not, why not? Should the text of these books be exegeted and then preached expositorily as we do John and the Psalms? Why not?

They want their experiences to be considered as reliable and true as Scripture - an actual divine revelation - but they do not want to suggest that they *are* Scripture. They speak as if their testimony is true and reliable and a real revelation from God, yet they avoid claims of infallibility and inerrancy. Likely neither man would suggest his book be regarded as an inspired 67th book after Revelation, yet that is the logical conclusion of their assertions. They can't have it both ways.

119

Either God is still speaking authoritatively, giving modern revelations of Heaven, or He is not. If He is, these are inerrant, infallible, and inspired texts. If He is not, these books are lies from the father of lies.

These accounts excuse people's unbelief of the clear testimony of Scripture. They satisfy a wicked and perverse generation's lust for sensationalistic tales. They promote self-contradictory and unbiblical notions of Heaven, Jesus, the Holy Spirit, the future, and inspired Scripture. They minimize the revelation God has given while promoting their own delusional experiences as if they are divine truth.

Conclusion

I do not expect the business of Heaven Tourism to come to a halt anytime soon. It is big business that offers celebrity status, large royalty checks, and movie deals. I anticipate that there will be more sensationalist claims in the future from more second-rate charlatans promising yet more information about the afterlife.

The discerning Christian will do the discerning thing: reject such claims outright. We can know with utmost certainty that they are lies. Anyone who dishonors, contradicts, and undermines Scripture the way these men do is no messenger from God. They are liars.

I do not know whether they are deceived themselves, or whether they are intentionally and knowingly lying, but I know they are lying. I do not need to know why a man is lying to know that he is lying. We can test their words against Scripture. We can examine their teachings. When we do, it is evident that these accounts are false.

Test all things. Hold fast to that which is true.

5

Do You Know the True Gospel?

If you purchased *Heaven Is for Real* or *90 Minutes in Heaven* in hopes of finding out **how** to get to Heaven, then you will be sorely disappointed. I have read and reread both of those books. While reading, I searched desperately for anything that even came close to a gospel presentation. There is none.

Don Piper and Todd Burpo both say they want people to believe that Heaven is real and they want people to go there. Piper even says that he feels compelled to make the way absolutely clear. Yet, sadly, neither man offers any explanation of the simple gospel truth.

So I ask you dear reader, "Do you know what the true gospel is?" Please allow me the privilege of sharing it with you.

"Gospel" means "good news." But before we can appreciate the good news, we need to understand the *bad news*.

The bad news is that nobody deserves to go to Heaven. In fact, all men deserve eternal, conscious torment in Hell for their sins. That may sound harsh, but only if you believe that you are actually a pretty good person. The truth is, we are not good people. This is evident most clearly when we compare ourselves to God's standard of goodness - His moral law. Have you ever stopped to compare yourself to the 10 Commandments and asked yourself if you have kept those commandments?

For instance, have you ever told a lie? Unless you have a hyper-inflated unrealistic view of yourself, you are going to answer that question with "yes." It does not matter how "small" the lie is from your perspective, or how innocent you deem the untruth to be, you have lied. That is a violation of the ninth commandment, "You shall not bear false witness" (Exodus 20:16). Even one lie makes you a liar in the sight of God. He has promised all liars that "their part will be in the lake that burns with fire and brimstone, which is the second death" (Revelation 21:8).

Have you ever stolen anything? Again, it does not matter if you deem it to be of little value. If you have ever taken anything that did not belong to you, then you are a thief. Stealing is a violation of the eighth Commandment, "You shall not steal" (Exodus 20:15).

Have you ever taken God's name in vain? Have you ever used God's name in the same way you would use a filthy four letter curse word to express disgust? Have you ever used the name of Jesus Christ in a way that does not honor Him? If you have, then you are guilty of blasphemy. That is a violation of the third commandment (Exodus 20:7), and a very serious crime. The Old Testament required the death penalty for someone in the nation of Israel who was found guilty of blasphemy. That is how seriously God takes the honor of His own name. The word of God says that "the LORD will not leave him unpunished who takes His name in vain."

Blasphemy is a serious crime! You have taken the name of the God who gave you life, and has showered you with kindness, and you have drug it through the mud and used it as if it is a common curse word. Blasphemy is an expression of one's hatred for God. What you would never think to do

122

to the name of Adolf Hitler, you do regularly to the name of the glorious and holy God.

One final question from the 10 Commandments: Have you ever committed adultery? There may be a number of people reading this who at first glance think that they have kept this commandment. But not so fast! Jesus said in Matthew 5:27–28, "You have heard that it was said, 'You shall not commit adultery'; but I say to you that everyone who looks at a woman with lust for her has already committed adultery with her in his heart." *Now* do you think you have kept the commandment?

Jesus said if you even lust after someone, or look on someone with sexual desire, you have violated that commandment. God does not just look on our actions, but He sees the desires and intentions of our heart. God examines our thought life. Our problem is not just that we sin in act, but in thought and word as well.

If God were to judge you by the standard of the 10 Commandments, would He find you "innocent" or "guilty" on the day of judgment? The answer is "guilty."

Since you would be found guilty on the day of judgment, what should a good, holy, and righteous God do to you? Should a righteous God let guilty sinners into Heaven, or should that just and righteous God send guilty sinners to Hell?

Notice that I did not ask you, "What do you **want** God to do with you on the day of judgment?" but, "What **should** a righteous judge do with you on the day of judgment?"

Don't we like to see justice done? We feel righteously indignant when murderers, rapists, or child molesters, go free on some legal technicality. We don't like to see guilty people go unpunished. There is something deep within all of us that desires that justice be done. We think that it is a travesty of justice if an earthly judge lets guilty lawbreakers go free. Likewise, it would not be right or just for God to simply wink at sin and let guilty sinners go unpunished. The just demands of the law must be met. Justice must be satisfied.

This is the bad news- that we are "all under sin" (Romans 3:9), all the world is guilty before God (Romans 3:19-20). **But** there is good news.

God is rich in mercy and grace, and has made a way whereby guilty sinners may enter Heaven. Jesus Christ, Who is God in human flesh, came into this world to die on a cross so that He might pay the penalty for the sins of all who will trust in Him. He lived a perfect life. He never sinned. He did fully the will of God and never transgressed the law of God in thought, word, or deed. He was perfectly righteous.

He lived a perfect life and died a perfect death. Jesus died on the cross to bear the wrath of the Father that we deserve (1 Peter 2:24-25). The Bible says that He "was pierced through for our transgressions, He was crushed for our iniquities; The chastening for our well-being fell upon Him, And by His scourging we are healed" (Isaiah 53:5). "But the Lord has caused the iniquity of us all to fall on Him" (Isaiah 53:6).

His death on the cross was no accident. He laid down His life for His sheep (John 10:11-18). He came to give His life as a ransom for many (Mark 10:45).

Three days after He died, He rose from the dead, never to die again. He was raised from the dead, the victorious conqueror of death, in a glorified body. His resurrection from the dead was proof that the Father approved of His sacrifice for sins, and that the wrath of the Father was satisfied on behalf of all those who trust the Son.

This is good news! The justice of God has been satisfied. Jesus Christ has offered a sacrifice sufficient to pay the price for your sin. His righteousness is infinitely sufficient to present you righteous before the throne of God on Judgment Day. He paid the debt so that you may go free.

God commands you to respond to this good news. He commands you to repent (Acts 17:30-31). To repent means that you agree with God that you are a sinner deserving of eternal judgment, and that you turn from sin and to the Lord Jesus Christ. Further, God commands you to believe upon the Lord Jesus Christ for salvation (Acts 16:31). Place your faith in Him. Believe that He died for you and that His sacrifice was the just payment for your sin. Trust in Him. Rest in Him and Him alone and His work on the cross on your behalf.

When you turn from sin and believe on the Lord Jesus Christ, you will be saved. You will be born again. God will give you a new heart with new desires. Through repentance and faith, we lay hold of the work of Christ on our behalf. It is by grace that you are saved through faith, and not by works (Ephesians 2:8-9). There is nothing you can do to earn eternal life. There is nothing you can do to atone for your sin, or reform your life. Salvation is a free gift which must be received by faith.

If you will not repent and believe upon Christ for salvation, then you will stand before the righteous judge who will judge you in righteousness for the crimes you have committed (Acts 17:30-31). You will stand before Him without a sin bearer, without anyone to pay your fine or bear your punishment. You will stand before Him clothed only in the filthy robes of your own self righteousness. You will stand before Him guilty and condemned and He will give you what you deserve.

125

Be reconciled to God! "He made Him who knew no sin to be sin on our behalf, so that we might become the righteousness of God in Him" (2 Corinthians 5:21). The promise of Jesus is: "Truly, truly, I say to you, he who hears My word, and believes Him who sent Me, has eternal life, and does not come into judgment, but has passed out of death into life" (John 5:24).

John 3:16 says, "For God so loved the world, that He gave His only begotten Son, that whoever believes in Him shall not perish, but have eternal life."

Believe upon the Lord Jesus Christ today!

About the Author

Jim Osman was born in May of 1972 and has lived in Sandpoint, Idaho since he was three years old. He graduated from Sandpoint High School in 1990. Jim came to know Christ through the ministry of Cocolalla Lake Bible Camp in the summer of 1987. Kootenai Community Church has always been his home church, attending Sunday School, Vacation Bible School and Youth Group.

After graduating from High School, Jim attended Millar College of the Bible in Pambrun, Saskatchewan. It was at Bible College that Jim met his wife-to-be, Diedre, who was also enrolled as a student. Jim graduated with a three year diploma in April of 1993 and married Diedre in August of that same year. He returned to Millar to further his education in September of 1994 and graduated from the Fourth Year Internship Program with a Bachelor of Arts in Strategic Ministries in April of 1995. He was inducted into the Honor Society of the Association of Canadian Bible Colleges and appointed a member of Pi Alpha Mu.

Jim and Diedre returned to Sandpoint where Jim began working in construction as a roofer until he was asked to take over as the preaching elder of Kootenai Community Church in December of 1996. Now he counts it his greatest privilege to be involved in ministering in the church that ministered to him for so many years.

Jim loves to be outdoors, whether it is camping, hunting, or working in his garden. He enjoys bike riding and watching football, especially his favorite team, the San Francisco 49ers, for whom he has cheered since childhood. Jim and Diedre have four children: Taryn, Shepley, Ayden and Liam. They are all 49er fans!

Jim is the author of Truth Or Territory: A Biblical Approach to Spiritual Warfare. You can contact Jim through Kootenai Community Church.

http://www.kootenaichurch.org
http://www.truthorterritory.com

Made in the USA
Columbia, SC
25 August 2023